MEN OF LEAD
MINERS OF THE YORKSHIRE DALES

DAVID JOY

Galena Books

Published by Galena Books
an imprint of Paradise Press Ltd
Scale Haw, Hole Bottom, Hebden, Skipton, BD23 5DL

ISBN: 978 0 9934923 0 3

British Library Cataloguing in Publication Data
A catalogue record for this book is available from
the British Library

Front cover by Andrew Cheetham

Line drawings except where otherwise credited are by
Les Turner, © Yorkshire Dales National Park Authority

Design and layout: Richard Joy

Printed by The Amadeus Press, Cleckheaton, West Yorkshire

CONTENTS

Robust repair work on a mine railway at Yarnbury, above Grassington.

Preface
and Acknowledgements

This book has had a protracted gestation. It origins go back more than 40 years to the time when I was books editor of the Dalesman and regularly met the late Arthur Raistrick, a leading authority on lead mining and miners as well as many other aspects of the Yorkshire Dales. At one such meeting in 1973 he made a characteristically forthright pronouncement: 'There is now available, in increasing numbers, books on lead mining. However, it is rare to find any direct reference to the conditions in which men worked or to the effect of their work on their health and their life. There is a need for serious research into the human aspects of every part of the lead miners' work.'

It was a statement that sparked a desire to write a book on such a theme, coupling the lives of lead miners with the way they changed key mining communities. Only recently did it prove possible to bring together material collected over the last four decades into a draft manuscript 'Lead Miners of the Yorkshire Dales'. This increasingly seemed an uninspiring title and also too similar to existing studies of mining. Fortunately, when Andrew Cheetham was preparing the striking cover illustration he suggested 'Men of Lead' as the main title. This immediately struck a chord and in today's phraseology has subsequently been described as 'sexier' than my original wording. It may not please all those interested in the subject but accords with a wish to create a non-specialist book of broad appeal. It has been self-published under the Galena imprint, taking its name from the natural mineral in which lead ore is found.

Some may be troubled by the lack of technical detail. A prime reason is the work of the Northern Mine Research Society [NMRS], which has met this need in both its memoirs and monographs, many of which are listed at the end of this book. Deeply researched and authoritative, I cannot commend them too highly.

Another cause of concern maybe the absence of referencing. That said, endnotes and footnotes can clutter the pages and will not be required by the majority of readers. Moreover, the age of the Internet means that those reading a book no longer need to be separated from its author in the way that was once the case. An annotated version of the text is therefore available by contacting me on: dawjoy@aol.com. As part of a two-way dialogue, I shall be pleased to receive comments and updates.

A final point on the text concerns money. To state that something cost say £50 in 1800 does not convey a great deal in present-day terms. All money values therefore include today's figure based on the percentage increase in the Retail Price Index. This is a controversial area and it cannot be stressed too highly that it is no more than an approximate indication.

Mike Gill, NMRS Recorder, has most helpfully devoted a great deal of time to reading and checking the text, while Helen Bainbridge of Swaledale Museum and Shirley Everett of Greenhow Local History Club have also commented on specific chapters. I am most grateful for their corrections and suggestions. All three have also assisted with the provision of illustrations, which has proved to be almost as challenging as the writing. Uncredited photographs are by the author or from his collection.

Images of lead miners at work are few and far between and no claim is made that those in this book are hitherto unpublished. Happily, their life and times were evocatively captured in a series of drawings by Les Turner, commissioned for a lead mining trail at Grassington by the Yorkshire Dales National Park Authority, which have been made available by Robert White, Senior Historic Environment Officer.

Art of a very different kind is represented by early portraits. It was a privilege when Charlie Yorke allowed me to photograph those of his ancestors back to Sir John Yorke, who played a fundamental role in Greenhow lead mining as early as the mid-16th century.

The death of mining put most villages in shock and a state of suspended animation with little immediate physical change. The legacy miners left behind was therefore captured on early postcards, and David Dean, Ben McKenzie and Clive Torrens have contributed images from their collections.

I hope that all concerned will enjoy seeing their efforts in print.

David Joy   *February 2016*

INTRODUCTION

Lead quickly tarnishes and becomes dull and grey but not so the saga of men who gave their all in searching for this most tantalising of riches. It may not have been mined to any extent for more than a hundred years, yet it remains a subject of perennial fascination. Small wonder – it has everything to excite the imagination.

Men versus danger has always been an enduring theme. It could have no better setting than deep underground with miners toiling in dank air by the dim light of flickering candles. Adding to the high drama was the fact that many mines were on wild and windswept moorland miles from anywhere. Dwellings were sometimes built close-by that were little more than hovels for miners and their families. Occasionally a small village would evolve where previously there had been nothing, but as the industry developed so did miners settle for what was often a long trudge to work and squeeze into existing settlements. Overcrowding became the norm, although here they could at least share their woes and poverty. Life was often short and reward meagre.

They could also gather in pubs and speculate endlessly on another theme that has made lead mining so fascinating. It was literally and metaphorically the chance of striking it rich in a constant search for buried treasure. The geology could scarcely have made the quest more challenging, as veins of lead ore in near vertical fault fissures were erratic in nature and completely unpredictable. In section they could be hundreds of feet deep yet only inches wide and rarely vertical. Length could vary from a few yards to several miles, but even when found they could curve all over the place. Moreover, the amount of lead ore within a vein was unknown and if the figure exceeded ten per cent it was a rich mine. A promising start could go barren with the temptation that it might resume and then get even better if the quest was pursued just that little bit further. It was so often an elusive dream, akin to finding a needle in an underground haystack.

The relentless quest by men who risked so much for so little might seem sufficient for any saga. Yet there was a further twist from the mid-18th century when the industrial revolution created an unprecedented demand for lead with random searches by farmer-miners giving way to outside expertise and investment. In an age where social divisions meant everything, miners as a whole came to be seen as the lowest orders of society, especially by the established church, and vastly more concern was focused on a very different kind of risk taken by the mine owners. Including a bizarre assemblage of wealthy aristocrats, they invested the present-day equivalent of millions. In some cases it can have been little different to seeking fortune on the gambling tables where so much of their time was spent. Big houses were built by the owners for themselves or their agents, which added to the 'Upstairs - Downstairs' nature of the mines and their men.

Like the best dramas, it all had a sudden ending – and in this case it was not a happy one. With lead being so challenging to find, it was necessary to spend ever more in going deeper in search of new reserves. All might have been well had not the advent of steamships enabled ore to be brought in from countries such as Spain at a lower cost. The resulting collapse soon after the high noon of the Victorian age was sudden and there was little alternative employment for miners in remote parts of the Yorkshire Dales. With much sorrow and suffering, they and their families had to leave an area that would never be quite the same again. Industry was replaced by silence and dereliction, and only a tiny part of its physical heritage now remains as a reminder of what was achieved against overwhelming odds.

It is scarcely surprising that more books may well have been written on lead mining in the Yorkshire Dales than any other subject. They include many excellent technical monographs and more extensive works that now cover all the main mining areas, but there is still relatively little on the miners themselves and the way they changed life in the Dales. Hence no apology is made for this social history, which approaches the subject in a different way. The first part looks at how the gradual development of mining affected those involved and the way they came to be divided into the separate roles of 'deadmen' doing preparatory work, miners toiling underground, dressers handling the ore brought out of the mine, smelters turning it into lead, and carriers transporting the finished product. It then goes on to portray the life of the men – their homes, health, religion, leisure (such as it was) and learning. It also attempts to correct an omission in most mining books – and that is any mention of women.

The second part examines key mining communities in the Dales, showing how villages that had once viewed miners as a shifting and feckless population now saw them bring transformation in their wake. It does not attempt to be comprehensive as the scattered nature of the industry meant that many villages had just a few miners among their population. Instead it

Miners sorting ore at No. 2 Shaft on Greenhow about 1910. The search for lead lasted longer here than in many parts of the Dales, in large measure due to ore being found at great depth when a pipeline was constructed from Scar House Reservoir to Bradford.

concentrates on those associated with the two major veins in the area. The long and rich Friarfold vein, which ran along the moors north of Swaledale all the way from above Keld to east of Arkengarthdale, had many shorter cross veins. Most of the nearby villages numbered a substantial proportion of miners and thus receive separate attention. The Bycliffe vein, which also had numerous offshoots, extended from the edge of Conistone Moor in Upper Wharfedale across to Greenhow Hill above Nidderdale. Apart from Greenhow itself, specifically created by miners, the key settlements were Grassington and Hebden – and each of the three was totally different.

Finally, there is a look at the small mining hamlet of Hole Bottom, north of Hebden. It might appear to be an ego trip, as it is where this book has been written and published. A possible excuse is that it stands out from the crowd as its three houses were homes to very different families – the Duke of Devonshire's mine agent, a succession of miners and ore dressers, and more than one generation of smelters. It has been included in recognition of the massively growing interest in family history and thus includes details of sources for those undertaking similar research. For the same reason there is a separate index of people, as it is they who are at the heart of a book on men of lead.

Horses would continuously walk in a circle to turn a 'whim' and lift spoil and ore up a shaft.

PART 1

1. MINERS DOWN THE AGES

Lead ingots dating from 81 A.D. have been found near Greenhow, showing that the Romans were searching for ore in the southern Dales almost two thousand years ago. Yet not until the 14th century is there any firm evidence of mineral extraction, when monastic times saw lead become highly valued for weatherproofing church roofs and as an essential part of stained glass windows. Monks at Fountains, Byland and Jervaulx Abbeys as well as Bolton Priory were soon aware of the potential importance of deposits in the Dales.

Veins would then outcrop in cliffs and rocks with little soil cover or in stream beds. They must have intrigued generations of Dales farmers venturing onto the high moors in search of stray sheep. When first exposed the lead would have an enticing silvery lustre, but initial excitement must have been tempered when it quickly became a dullish blue-grey with great weight its most distinguishing feature.

With monastic encouragement the farmers would no doubt start extracting the ore. It would at first involve no more than digging trenches or sinking shallow pits, often in rows surrounded by spoil and resembling giant molehills. The quest would be haphazard and prone to interruption during lambing or haymaking or extremes of weather. Yet in those harsh times success could make the difference between destitution and survival. Once found the ore would be smelted in primitive hearths known in the Dales as 'bales', which consisted of little more than low stone walls lined with clay. They were placed on exposed hillsides, often facing the prevailing south-westerly wind so that the draft would raise the temperature of the fire sufficiently to form molten lead.

The importance of the mineral was recognised by the sixteenth century historians John Leland and William Camden, who noted that 'the hills afford great store of lead'. As demand increased, many new owners who had acquired great swathes of land following dissolution of the monasteries found themselves to be in a favoured position. They would allow farmers to become farmer-miners, forming partnerships working

Inclined level at Yarnbury, completed in 1828 just as the price of lead fell drastically and resulted in a first wave of emigration.

strips of ground in return for retaining a fraction of the ore raised.

Activity increased with shallow digs along the projected course of a vein turning into deeper pits and often using a rope drum or 'inverted whim' turned round and round by one or more horses. Boys were taken underground to convey ore to the foot of the shaft, from where it was hauled to the surface in wooden or iron buckets ('kibbles') using a hand windlass locally called a 'jack roller'. Water was also generally removed in the same way, although sometimes it would be lifted in leather bags.

In remote and hilly places where damage was not a consideration, there was the more spectacular process of hushing with reservoirs being built above the place to be worked. The dam was then breached in expectation that the sudden flush of water would expose any veins. Success was far from certain.

Such methods more or less met demand until it came to the industrial revolution of the mid-18th century. By now most ore close to the surface had been extracted and a fundamental change was needed to meet a sudden demand for lead, not just in the mill towns of the West Riding and Lancashire but more generally for roofing, glazing, plumbing, munitions and paint. A new era of mining deeper underground would involve more than just local knowledge and would also cost serious money. These requirements were met by mining experts and industrialists from outside

John Taylor 1779 - 1863 (left), the 'Father of British Mining', who was brought in by the 6th Duke of Devonshire 1790 - 1858 (right) to act as his agent. The result was a revolution in mining operations at Grassington. (National Portrait Gallery)

the Dales, while at the same time the area became attractive to venture capitalists then known as Adventurers. Fortunes were made – and lost.

Much now depended on the owner of the mineral rights, who was often quite separate from the landowner. He was frequently a wealthy absentee landlord, who would seek to maximise income at minimum risk by a straightforward lease of the minerals in return for receiving a rent and a royalty on all lead produced. Exceptions were in the minority but could be spectacular. When the mineral rights at Grassington were inherited by the 6th Duke of Devonshire, he brought in John Taylor – the greatest mining engineer of his day – to act as his agent. The present-day equivalent would be a chief executive of international stature transforming a slumbering enterprise within a matter of weeks.

A standard practice was now a system of 'bargaining', whereby partnerships would negotiate with owners, agents or lessees to work a stretch of vein for a given price per weight of ore raised. This price varied greatly according to the anticipated richness of the vein and ease of extracting the

Fortunes were made and lost in the heyday of lead mining with protracted legal argument over mineral rights often being ruinously expensive. A series of partnership disputes in the early 18th century culminated in John Blackburne losing this magnificent home at Friar's Head near Winterburn.

ore, with adjustments being made at the end of the month or quarter. In effect payment by results, it rarely amounted to a 'bargain' in today's sense of the word. It was a system more likely to bring distress in its wake, as it was possible to work for long periods with little or no reward.

Despite its drawbacks, 'bargaining' survived as it encouraged initiative and hard work as well as preserving a degree of independence. It may not have been wholly an evolutionary process but it did come to the notice of Charles Darwin who was moved to comment: 'Where the system of selling part of the vein is followed, the miners, from being obliged to think and act for themselves, are a singularly intelligent and well-conducted set of men.' Others noted that miners remained 'generally subservient and of cap-touching loyalty'.

As in so many facets of more recent times, there were now cycles of sudden growth followed by severe depression. Halcyon years in the mid-18th century gave way to decline, partly due to disruption in foreign trade caused first by the American War of Independence and then the wars with France. Following the battle of Waterloo in 1815, there was again hardship when the price of lead dropped but three years later it recovered and remained consistently high for the next decade. Then came the inevitable recession, augmented by a reduction of import tariffs, when prices paid for lead fell by over a third within four years from the 1828 figure of £17 [£1,200] per ton.

Miners were among the first to join the tide of those seeking fortune elsewhere. Many went to Lancashire – and especially the Burnley area – to work in the collieries. It seemed there would also be employment for their families in the mills with their insatiable demand for child labour, although they soon found that conditions were little better as the cotton trade was also seriously affected. Others bravely headed to America, where a favoured destination was Wisconsin with its potential to combine lead mining with farming. Horrifying accounts were penned of heading out of Liverpool on month-long voyages in sailing ships, which were crowded with rows of bunks full of baggage and food as well as men, women and children coping badly with violent Atlantic gales.

High noon in mining communities in the 1850s brought new and welcome facilities in many villages. This reading room was attached to the end of a house in Grassington. (David Dean collection)

Some may soon have regretted such a move, as recovery at home was clearly evident by the mid-1830s. The California gold rush of 1849 nevertheless triggered further emigration, but only four years later the Crimean War took the price of lead to record levels. It was high noon in the mining communities and the resulting wealth brought new schools, libraries and reading rooms, Methodist chapels and Sunday schools. It spawned greater numbers of blacksmiths, carpenters, shoemakers, butchers, bakers and perhaps even candlestick makers.

Yet by the 1860s it was again clear that lead mining was in decline. Attempts were made to open up deeper reserves by driving long drainage levels through barren rock, as had successfully been done thirty years earlier with the Yarnbury and Grassington Moor mining field. It was a lengthy and expensive process requiring great faith by investors – and unfortunately it now came too late. In 1880 the only such level in Swaledale was completed in Gunnerside Gill after sixteen years of hard labour but never remotely justified its cost. Fifteen years were spent on a similar venture at Hebden before work was abandoned as late as 1888.

By this time gradual decline had turned into catastrophe, with the price of lead halving from £22 [£1,850] per ton to £11 in the ten years from 1875. At first there were faint hopes that it was a re-run of events in the early 1830s but it soon became apparent that the good times were not going to return. The coming of steamships heralded the dawn of globalisation. In what was to become a familiar story with so much of Britain's industry, it proved impossible to compete with countries extracting massive deposits of lead ore by cheap labour. At the same time exports were affected by economies of scale in America, which was now able to trade with distant markets that had previously been major UK customers.

Lead mining in the Dales on any meaningful scale was over and few emerged unscathed. Taking a long look back, high among those who had done best at least risk were lawyers of national standing, who must have made a fortune. Aggrieved parties were constantly going to law over a mineral that may have been grey but had the allure of gold and was responsible for many a bitter dispute. Middlemen in the shape of merchants also did well, but for most others it was a different story. Much had been invested and then lost by owner-operating enterprises, and it was perhaps inevitable that the great houses and country seats of those directly responsible came to be seen as a violent contrast to the poverty-stricken dwellings of their miners. Many a homestead became empty and many a village deserted, and it was to take a long time to dispel the era of doom that so rapidly descended.

2. MEN AT WORK

Deadmen

Lead mining came to involve increasing amounts of preparation and construction before a single piece of ore could be extracted. It was often done by miners who would agree a special price for what was called dead work. When this task was undertaken by those who did nothing else, they were termed 'deadmen'. It might seem an unfortunate and derogatory description, but they were only dead in the metaphorical sense of producing no direct revenue.

Where veins were cut by steep-sided valleys, as was often the case in Swaledale, it was possible to drive tunnels into the hillside. The portal was framed in well-built masonry, commonly arched and sometimes with an inscribed or dated keystone. Stone arching or timbering was used inside until either sound rock or the vein was reached. Normal dimensions were some 6ft 6in high by 4ft 6in wide in order to accommodate a narrow gauge railway on which pit ponies could bring ore out of the mine in wheeled wagons known as tubs. Although usually termed levels, these tunnels were in fact slightly inclined to enable water to drain away. The effort required by a pony to bring loaded tubs downgrade was therefore about the same as returning upgrade with empties. This made it easier for the person leading the pony, who could be a boy as young as ten and paid only ninepence [£1.20] a day. At least such work involved movement and was better than the common alternative of sitting in darkness and constantly turning a hand-operated fan – evocatively termed a 'windy king' – in an attempt to ventilate the mine.

Driving a level was arduous work for deadmen, especially if hard rock was encountered, but more demanding was the situation that developed on moor tops such as Grassington and Greenhow. Shafts that had once been relatively shallow had now to be sunk to depths of several hundred feet, much of the work being done by a 'whim' powered by horses walking round it in a circle. The same method was used to lower pit props into the mine and bring out the ore.

Shafts would frequently intersect levels and then go even deeper. Pumps and mechanical winding gear were installed to lift water from the more

Mine levels were normally of sufficient dimensions to enable wagons hauled by pit ponies to enter them. Stang Level, close to the road from Arkengarthdale to Barnard Castle, is seen here about 1909. (James Backhouse, per M.C. Gill)

intestinal reaches of the mine up to the level, from where it could run out to the surface by gravity. There was a certain irony that such essential drainage involved a constant supply of water! The winding gear was powered by massive waterwheels as much as 30 feet in diameter, fed by reservoirs that could often be miles distant. Clay or flag-lined watercourses would be skilfully surveyed, often seeming to flow uphill as they could have a fall of no more than fifty feet in half a mile. Only occasionally were steam engines introduced, a feature of Dales lead mining being the absence of any vast change when compared with more dynamic developments in the textile industry.

Waterwheels also powered increasingly mechanised dressing floors, laid out close to the mine to process the ore, as well as bellows inside the smelt mills. This all involved additional preparatory work, as did the need for blacksmith's shops to look after the hoofs of pit ponies and horses as well as tool shops to house essential mining equipment. A common necessity was adept use of stone. It was fortunate that development of the mines often coincided with enclosure of open moorland by many miles of drystone walls, meaning that gangs of skilled men were readily available. They were used to toiling through fair weather and foul, digging for the right stone and then speedily erecting walls without the use of mortar.

Dead work in the form of drystone walling is taking place at Yarnbury in front of the blacksmith's shop, close to which are the mine offices. Heading off to work are a miner and his young lad, who would probably have left school at the age of ten.

Miners

Although 'miners' remained a generic term for all those involved in the industry, it was the men who went underground that have always been closest to hazard and high drama. To distinguish them from those working on the surface, they were often termed 'groovers' or 'pickmen' – an allusion to constant use of a pickaxe.

Their work involved disappearing into a black hole, out of sight with all the uncertainties that this could bring. They once largely supervised themselves and decided their own hours, but had to face difficult times when a new breed of mine owners investing considerable capital demanded longer hours and constantly watched their costs. Working eight-hour shifts five days a week became common practice. Although later reduced to six hours, this took no account of the time taken to get to and from the mine.

Those employed by partnerships could be paid as little as ten shillings [£36] a week and then subjected to cost control that seems miserly beyond belief. Miners would call at the tool shop to collect their picks, shovels, hammers and hand drills, which in some cases were weighed by the company before being issued. After a fixed period, often once a month, they were weighed again and the miner was then charged for the amount of steel lost. The men also had to pay for gunpowder as well as candles, which were used in vast quantities and for many years were priced at 7d [95p] per pound.

Explosives for use inside the mine are brought out of a powder house. Such buildings were normally sited in an isolated location for obvious reasons.

They wore clothes considered best for the harsh conditions, with corduroy trousers or woollen breeches being purchased from travelling pedlars. Loose neckbands and coarse flannel shirts next to the skin were the norm. A moleskin coat might also be donned, sometimes with a tail tapering to a point much like the blade of a round-mouth shovel. In days long before waterproofs, the idea was that water constantly dripping onto the back would run off clear of the legs. This only worked to a limited extent and thus long stockings without feet, known as 'loughrams', were especially popular with miners. Worn on top of other clothes, they gave something on which to kneel and the oily nature of unwashed wool meant they helped to turn the wet.

In a miner's pockets could be an alarming combination of matches, gunpowder and tobacco for a clay pipe. Danger was part of the course, although at least a wide-brimmed hat in thick felt formed an apology for a safety helmet. Once the mine was reached, candles would be lit and carefully inserted into blacksmith-made lanterns. Not only did they bring a glimmer into the inky darkness but, should the light grow dim, they also forewarned of bad air. If the mine entrance was a shaft, there could be a descent of hundreds of feet on ladders with wooden stages providing a pause for breath. It was perhaps fortunate that the chasm below was invisible in the blackness.

Entry by a long level was likely to be less arduous, especially if it was possible to ride to the working area in tubs pulled by a pit pony. All concept

Miners drilling holes into a rock face, with one about to take careful aim with a hammer. Conditions were far more dark and dangerous than this photograph might suggest. (Beamish Museum)

of distance and space was soon lost and the only sounds were the drip-drip of water and men's footfalls splashing through mud that was everywhere.

Miners preferred to work upwards so that ore would fall rather than have to be lifted. They created rough shafts known as 'rises' to tap the near vertical veins of lead and a series of floors, which provided support for wooden ladders and held the 'deads' or waste material. Men generally worked in pairs to drill deep holes into the rock face. One miner held the hand drill and the other bashed it ferociously with a sledge hammer. Constant fear must have been part of the course as careful aim was needed in the near darkness. They would swap roles from time to time and when enough holes were drilled they would be filled with gunpowder. Fuses might be nothing more than paper or straw, but once lit the men retreated to a safe distance.

With luck the powder brought down far more rock than could mere wedges – at the expense of fouling the air with smoke and fumes. The discomforts of the choking atmosphere were dismissed with contempt, just as all the inherent dangers of the mine were scarcely given a thought. Always uppermost in the mind was a belief that the promised land in the form of an unbelievably rich vein of lead could lie just a few yards ahead.

Miners had a hunting instinct which drove them in quest of fresh quarry and made them unusually wary and alert. They also had a profound belief in the supernatural, hardly surprising when every shape was distorted by flickering lantern light and the movement of rocks created uncanny noises. They were always on the look out for 'little folk' – gnomes, boggles, spirits, fairies and hobgoblins – who once seen would supposedly direct miners to the richest deposits. If faint knocking sounds were heard then all work had to cease for the day, for it was said these were made by the ghosts of men killed in the mine and were a forewarning of imminent disaster. In reality they were probably caused by pockets of air. Despite such superstitions, serious accidents were relatively rare and only occasionally did excessive amounts of carbon dioxide from blasting result in fatalities.

There was one consolation. The mine might be dark, damp and dangerous but at least it was never freezing. The temperature underground varied little throughout the year and in winter could seem quite warm.

Dressers
Men emerging from a mine at the end of a shift would walk past those labouring on the dressing floors in very different conditions. Dressers were exposed to the weather's full severity and in winter their work was harsh in the extreme. It involved getting constantly splashed if not soaked and it was impossible to keep either dry or warm. Little attempt was made

Only in the closing days of mining did dressing floors have the luxury of a roof to keep out extreme weather. Here work is in progress at Harris Shaft on Greenhow Hill about 1890, with a bucker being used to crush ore on the right before it is placed in hotching tubs at left.

to cover dressing floors with any form of roof until the closing years of mining – and even then it was primarily to protect machinery that had a higher value than those employed there.

Working methods inside the mine never changed fundamentally, but this was not the case with ore dressing where a hand process of sorting and crushing gradually became mechanised. Where and when and to what extent this happened depended on the size of the enterprise, with the larger mines introducing centralised dressing floors serving several interlinked shafts or levels.

Typically, material emerging from the mine – and known as 'bouse' – was first tipped into 'bouse-teams', where output from each partnership was kept separately. Pieces of ore obvious by their weight and colour were put to one side ready for smelting but most material was taken to a grate. Here it was raked in a stream of water to clean it and enable more hand picking to take place. The remaining bouse was then crushed, initially by backbreaking work involving the use of flat-faced hammers ('buckers') on stone anvils ('knockstones'). This was superseded by grinding mills, tremendously noisy contraptions powered by a waterwheel and resembling a giant mangle. They could produce 50 tons of lead per day and enabled poor quality veins to be worked profitably.

After being crushed to pieces once regarded as between the size of a big pea

Ore being tipped into bouse-teams, where the output of each partnership working in the mine was kept separately.

Hand-operated hotching tubs, where the heavier ore was separated from waste by being jerked up and down in a sieve.

and a big broad bean, the material was put in a square sieve and suspended from hangars in a 'hotching tub'. The sieve was then jerked up and down in a tank of water, which again was initially done by hand but in later years involved rods connected to the waterwheel by eccentrics. Heavier ore sank to the bottom of the sieve and the waste was left on top to be removed to a 'dead' heap. Various further processes resulted in the ore being dressed to something like three-quarters of its lead content and then taken to the smelt mill.

It must have been a fascinating chain of work to see in action – and it was certainly labour intensive. It also depended entirely on waterpower and thus could be stopped for long periods in winter if watercourses became frozen. The only remedy was for men to take to the high moors armed with pickaxes and attempt to break the ice. Their efforts were often futile and the more exposed dressing floors routinely closed from December to March.

Smelters

The trials and tribulations of smelters were at the opposite extreme to those of ore dressers, as they were constantly wrestling with high temperatures rather than damp cold. Working with great heat on the face and a cold draught on the back of the neck, they would frequently compromise by wearing a thick knitted shawl that only covered the shoulders. They kept to themselves and were prepared to cope with working in smelt mills that were foul places emitting heavy fumes bad for human health. Their life expectancy was between eight and ten years less than the average miner with son routinely succeeding father at a depressingly early age.

Smelters were dedicated to their craft. They may not have understood the complex chemical reactions involved but they certainly knew by instinct such matters as correct fire temperatures and the proportion of good and poor ore to be used. The process generally took place in ore hearths resembling a blacksmith's forge.

A smelt began by placing bricks of peat, about a foot long by three inches square, on the cold hearth. Once lit a few shovelfuls of coal were thrown onto the peat and massive waterwheel-driven bellows were used to bring the mixture to the required temperature. The crushed ore was scattered on top, from which moment the smelter's skills came into play. Long pokers were used to move the ore to various parts of the fire where the right conditions for roasting were to be found. The desired temperature also had to be achieved by careful control of the blast from the bellows. At about 750° C the molten lead would trickle down into a sumpter pot, from where it could be ladled or tapped into moulds to form ingots known as 'pieces'.

This work would be repeated more than a dozen times and a smelting

Inside a smelt mill with two ore hearths as molten lead is poured from ladles into moulds. (Beamish Museum)

shift would produce somewhere between two and four tons of lead. Most mines had their own smelt mill, which would only be used when sufficient supplies of ore had been prepared at the dressing floors. The basic design, which remained little changed for some 350 years, was ideal for intermittent work of this kind. Ore hearths were almost universal in the Dales, although there was occasional adoption of reverberatory furnaces that performed best if worked continuously. These kept the ore separate from the fire with the heat being reflected – or 'reverberated' – off a specially shaped roof.

Mills had many associated activities involving men other than smelters. They had to look after the peat house and coal yard as well as checking and weighing the lead ready for dispatch.

Carriers

Finding ore and eventually producing lead was demanding enough, but it was not the final challenge. The product then had to be got to markets, which by the late 16th century were as distant as London and European ports. The sheer remoteness of the Yorkshire Dales made this especially difficult. It depended on carriers, who would be only too familiar with the old adage 'as heavy as lead'. They at first used packhorses, known as galloways, which were led over trackless fells in strings of at least twelve audible at great distance by the tinkling of bells. Each animal carried two pieces of lead weighing some 20 stones (125 kilograms) and would be on the hoof for several days. Leading the ponies was probably the healthiest job in the entire mining industry. It was necessary to reach a navigable waterway, which in the case of the southern dales was generally the River Ure at Boroughbridge, from where it was taken down the Ouse and Humber for transshipment at Hull. With Swaledale it involved an even longer journey to the mouth of the River Tees at Stockton.

Not until the late 18th century was there any significant change when output from many mines was outstripping the ability of packhorses to transport it. The result was the building of turnpikes, predecessors of today's toll roads, with mine owners often contributing much of the required capital for these privately funded ventures. Contact with the outside world was also eased following completion in 1773 of the Ripon Canal and then four years later the Leeds & Liverpool Canal as far as Skipton. Swaledale remained isolated until opening of a railway to Richmond in 1846, a year before completion of a line to Skipton. A final development in 1862 was a railway to Pateley Bridge, close to the Greenhow mines, although in this case it was rather too late in the day and decline was already underway.

Apart from handling lead, carriers were involved in numerous other tasks. Stores and timber had to be brought to the mines and peat and coal to the smelt mills. Their crucial role tends to be overlooked, but they were just as important as today's lorry drivers, be it long-distance or short-haul.

The coming of railways greatly helped the transport of lead – and especially so in Swaledale where carriers previously had to make a lengthy journey to Stockton-on-Tees. Pieces of lead are being individually weighed on primitive scales at Richmond station about 1870. (Ken Hoole collection, Darlington Railway Museum)

3. LIFE OF THE MINERS

Dalesmen

Men may have been divided into such 'trades' as miners, dressers or smelters, but they still had one feature in common. They were nearly all dalesmen – and thus definitely a breed apart. Harsh surroundings, climatic extremes and virtual isolation from the outside world led to extreme self-sufficiency and unswerving convictions.

They were always prone to understatement with 'not so bad' being the nearest they ever came to 'good'. Showing emotion was invariably avoided but beneath the surface was a generous spirit, deep sense of humour and love of hospitality. What was often dismissed as obstinacy hid intense local pride and a limpet-like determination to stay in their native dale. In the last days of mining it meant that life really had to be grim before they would accept the inevitable and leave their homeland. Constant struggle to survive also made them hard bargainers, which must have tried many a mine agent when negotiating terms.

Spinning a good yarn came easy to miners. After a pint or three of strong ale in one of the many pubs they would regale all within earshot of the 'El Dorado' just around the corner. They were going to strike the richest of ore within a matter of days and be rescued from absolute poverty – or so they believed! Such hopes were all too often essential, as it was common practice through much of the 18th century that miners were only paid quarterly or even half-yearly. Between times they were forced to live on credit, putting shopkeepers and other traders at risk. When payday finally came, it could result in a drinking bout lasting several days and set off a mounting spiral of debt. Poverty was at one time commonplace — and it was especially hard for their families. There was then no alternative but to seek help from the local Overseer of the Poor, who would often be a churchwarden with little sympathy for miners. Money was distributed with care verging on frugality and recipients had to suffer the indignity of seeing their household goods confiscated and sold.

Those in dire straits were moved to 'poorhouses', which were opened in many villages and were forerunners of the notorious workhouses of Victorian times. Here conditions resembled a prison, with men separated

Bringing peat down from the moor by horse and cart was a family occupation. It would either be burnt at home or sometimes sold to the nearest smelt mill.

from their wives, forced to wear uniform, fed minimum amounts of food and consigned to menial tasks such as breaking stone. Small wonder that poverty became a terrible stigma to be avoided at all costs. Inmates must have envied fellow dalesmen who had escaped incarceration – and especially those who were combining lead mining with the outdoor life of a farmer.

Farmer-Miners

Men lucky enough to have a smallholding could work at the mine from around 8.0am through to early afternoon and then have the rest of the day to tend their fields and livestock. It was a system that generally worked well, although the noted agriculturalist Arthur Young lamented in 1770 that it left 'half a day for idleness, or rioting in the alehouse'.

Farm life was ruled by the Dales climate with its short growing season and almost unbearably long winter. Favourite sound of the farm year was the March call of the curlew, a harbinger that spring was just around the corner and sheep grazing on the open fell would be gathered close to the farmhouse for lambing.

Going onto the moor in spring to cut peat was a family ritual. Men dug the peat and then women and children helped to carry it to firm dry ground, where it would be stacked conically to dry over the next three to four months. It would then be loaded into carts and either brought home or sold to the nearest smelt mill.

Cattle providing all-essential milk were turned out of their shippons in May. A farmer-miner would commonly have just a single cow, which was so important that insurance schemes were eventually started to cover the cost of a replacement in case of accident or disease. Sheep washing took place in late June followed about ten days later by shearing.

A typical size for a smallholding was only eight acres (3.25 hectares) but those who had enough land would grow hay, which was cut by hand with scythes and then strewn in the field to dry. It was an arduous task that had to be repeated time and time again if it rained. The necessity for much manual labour was met by hiring less fortunate miners with no land of their own, who were only too glad for a spell in fresh air and sunny meadows. It came to be regarded as an annual unpaid holiday of two or three weeks' duration.

If the weather held, bracken was then cut on the fell, dried to avoid poisoning the stock and stored to be used as bedding for the coming winter. Another routine chore at this time of year was salving sheep with a mixture of oils, fats and tar to kill parasites and prevent scab. All too soon it was winter and the dull routine of shorter days with milking, foddering and muck shifting frequently having to take place in total darkness. On the bleakest of nights it must have seemed far worse than going down the mine. Despite such conditions, the demand for land was high and rents could soar to excessive levels. Miners felt a smallholding could provide a degree of certainty never found in a vein of lead.

Women
The life of a miner's wife was by today's standards unbelievably hard. She would frequently have to endure rather than enjoy many years of almost ceaseless procreation in an age when infant mortality was high. Several of her offspring could indeed die young but equally they might all survive. Families of ten children, produced in fifteen years and somehow crammed into a two-bedroom home, were not uncommon. It must have been a relief when they could be sent to what passed for a school, although this could be short-lived in the days before compulsory education. Boys would scarcely have absorbed the three Rs when they left to work at the mines aged ten or even eight, with the result that a large proportion of the male population was illiterate. In the southern dales, girls would from the 1790s be dispatched to work at the newly-built textile mills.

Daily chores to be undertaken in the home included laying and lighting fires, boiling water, cooking, washing pots, cleaning, more cooking, filling warming pans for the beds, and so on and so on. Rushes dipped in melted

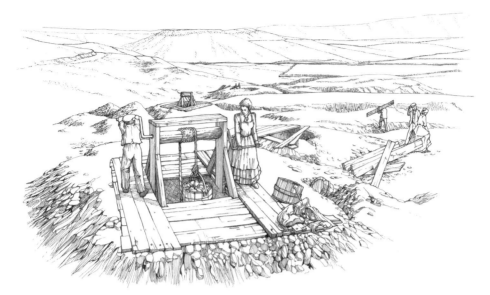

Women did not work underground in the lead mines but they did help with such tasks as hauling ore out of shafts by means of 'jack rollers'.

tallow formed the only means of lighting until the introduction of oil lamps, although even then a lot of time had to be devoted to trimming wicks.

The dangers of lead were not fully recognised and so extensive use was made of local utensils. During butter making, milk was placed in lead bowls to allow the cream to rise. It was then scraped off the sides of the bowl after draining away the skimmed milk, which in turn was used to make cheese that had the drawback of becoming so hard that it had to be toasted over a candle.

Prepared on an almost daily basis was havercake, which was hung to dry on a special rack. Potatoes were consumed in great quantity and other food included dumplings, mutton and offal boiled to form soup, augmented by bacon among those fortunate enough to keep a pig. Oatmeal was once used extensively but came to be considered by miners as 'too heating' and gave way to tea and coffee. It was an age of self-sufficiency and any opportunity to pick bilberries and blackberries growing wild would not be missed.

Apart from daily tasks there was also a weekly routine. On Fridays the stone-flagged floors would be washed and sprinkled with sand, obtained by braying pieces of sandstone with the same sort of bucker used on the dressing floors. In the evening it was bath night with extra water being boiled to fill a big tub placed in front of the fire. Next day the floors were swept and rugs and matting put down in readiness for Sunday and a brief moment of

31

relaxation on returning from chapel. Cleanliness came next to godliness, so Monday was washing day. Clothes were 'pegged' in a big tub and put through a mangle of almost bone-crushing ferocity before being hung out to dry.

Essential supplies would be bought weekly at the village market when all and sundry would converge from the surrounding district on horseback. A special annual event was a fair, when yearly accounts were settled, as ready money was then a rare commodity. For once it was possible to escape constant work and there was much revelry with more than adequate refreshment.

Menfolk would hopefully help with such seasonal tasks as salting beef and pork, emptying ash pits, spring cleaning and, twice a year, lime-washing the walls with a cream-like mixture formed by 'slaking' – pouring water onto a cob of lime in a bucket.

Women commonly worked underground in collieries, but there is no truth in the enduring legend that this was also the case in lead mines. They certainly helped family income by using 'jack rollers' to haul ore out of shafts, sorting through spoil heaps and providing much of the labour on dressing floors, working in small groups supervised by a master washer. Out in all weathers meant that crippling rheumatism was commonplace. Had equal pay been an issue, something might have been said in 1720 when one mine was paying women 4d [£2.25] a day and its miners could be receiving up to 1s 2d [£7.75].

Such practices lasted well into the 19th century. When the Rev Benjamin Newton, Rector of Wath, visited Arkengarthdale in 1817 he was moved to note in his diary: 'Saw some very handsome girls washing the lead.' Quite what swayed such emotions is intriguing, as village dress in the form of a bonnet and a wincey frock would be abandoned in favour of more durable clothing such as a heavy flannel petticoat.

Mechanisation of dressing floors gradually brought change, although ironically it meant there was less work for women – and hence a reduced source of family income – at a time when the industry was at its height. A new attitude was evident in 1857 when a visitor to Old Gang mines in Swaledale took the moral high ground: 'Young women are engaged at working at the hotching tubs, and this is a matter of regret, because the employment of women in hard out-of-door work always implies a want of social refinement.'

Homes
There is no equivalent in the Dales of long rows of brick-built terraces, which even today are such a feature of settlements in South Yorkshire once dedicated to coal mining. When dalesmen tilling the land and

tending livestock became farmer-miners, they continued to live in simple dwellings as had traditionally been the case. In the well-wooded southern dales these would generally be cruck-framed buildings, using slightly curved tree trunks erected to meet at the top and held together by a collar beam, roughly in the shape of a letter 'A'. Pairs of crucks were joined by a horizontal roof-tree to form a timber framework. Low walls were constructed of stone or 'wattle and daub' consisting of intertwined branches plastered with clay or mud. The roof was ling thatch and the floor either flagstones or beaten earth. Smoke from an open-hearth fire was all pervading and mingled with the smell of body odour to create an aroma far from fragrant.

In the more northern dales with a shortage of suitable timber, the dwellings were often single storey and had a close affinity to the Norse 'long house'. There would be a single living area, one or two bedrooms and under the same roof might be a cow byre and space for fodder. A roof of turf or ling thatch rested on rubble walls as was also the case with separate cowsheds in adjacent fields.

Dissolution of the monasteries and a new age of prosperous manorial landlords or yeomen led to a great rebuilding lasting through much of

Most miners crowded into existing dwellings in established villages, as here in Grassington's Main Street. This photograph is thought to date from 1898, less than 20 years after closure of the local lead mines, so it is scarcely surprising that this row was still known as "the miners' cottages". (David Dean collection)

the 17th and early 18th centuries. Many new houses in stone were of generous proportions with plenty of space, which came into its own with the expansion of mining. Properties were often divided in two with the owner letting one half to a mining family. Typical rents in the mid-19th century ranged widely from 10s [£50] to £2 [£200] per year.

Where terraces were constructed or infilling took place, the materials were of local stone that today has assimilated well into the vernacular architecture. Smaller dwellings that had remained single-storey were extended upwards to create first-floor living space and rooms were also provided over stables. Furniture was basic and generally comprised little more than a table, some chairs, a chest of drawers and the odd cupboard, with beds being crammed together several to a room. Some miners were lucky enough to have a grandfather clock, although it could easily represent the equivalent of six months' wages.

Below: Dwellings built by farmer-miners in the more remote locations were primitive structures with thatched roofs. One of the last such buildings was photographed in 1942 at Hurst in Swaledale. (Clive Torrens collection)
Opposite, top: Prior to its demolition six years later this same cottage was surveyed by Robert Clough when compiling his seminal book The Lead Smelting Mills of the Yorkshire Dales.
Lower: *Cowsheds at remote locations such as Hurst also retained the same tradition of rubble wall and thatch (survey by James Walton, 1946).*

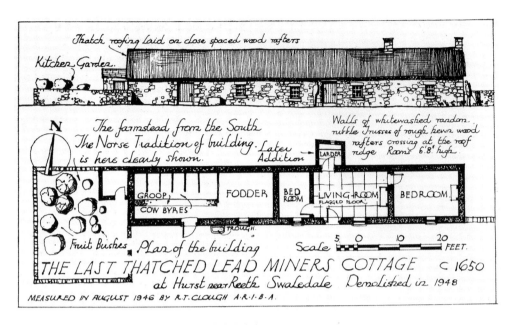

Thatch roofing laid on close spaced wood rafters

Kitchen Garden.

N

The farmstead from the South
The Norse Tradition of building. Later
is here clearly shown. Addition

Walls of whitewashed random
rubble Trusses of rough hewn wood
rafters crossing at the roof
ridge Rooms 6'8" high.

LARDER

GROOP
COW BYRES

FODDER

BED
ROOM

LIVING ROOM
FLAGGED FLOOR

BEDROOM

TROUGH.

Fruit Bushes Plan of the building

Scale 5 0 10 20 FEET.

THE LAST THATCHED LEAD MINERS COTTAGE c 1650
at Hurst near Reeth Swaledale Demolished in 1948

MEASURED IN AUGUST 1946 BY R.T.CLOUGH A·R·I·B·A·

Primitive Cowshed HURST

Scale 0 5 10 15 20 feet

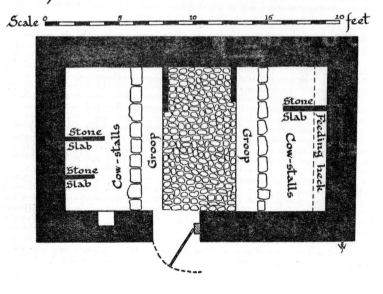

Stone Slab

Stone Slab

Cow-stalls

Groop

Groop

Stone Slab

Cow-stalls

Feeding heck

35

Conditions could at times become decidedly cramped and unhealthy, although they were seldom as bad as those in many mill towns. They were at their worst in the relatively few dwellings built away from villages close to the mine workings. These tended to be little more than hovels with poor-quality stonework, tiny windows and totally inadequate for the weather on an exposed hillside.

Health

As lead was an elusive mineral and work was governed by the hope of untold riches, the gambling spirit triumphed over any considerations of health. Life could be very short indeed, owing to various respiratory diseases popularly known as 'miner's consumption'. These were accentuated by working in badly ventilated and damp conditions prior to walking home with wet clothes and footwear. In July 1857 the depressing mortality rate attracted attention in the august Journal of the British Medical Association. Dr Thomas Jackson of Darlington listed chronic conditions such as rheumatic fever and bronchial illnesses including congestion and inflammation of the lungs. Treatments ranged from warm baths and absolute rest through to inducing vomiting by means of ipecacuanha – the dried root of a plant from Brazil. The good doctor noted but did not condemn the practice of miners constantly smoking in the belief that it was 'most beneficial' in bringing up phlegm and thus relieving difficulties in breathing.

Thomas Dunham Whitaker, cleric and author in 1805 of the scholarly two-volume History of Craven. *He despised miners with an intensity that can only have helped the spread of Methodism in the Dales.*

At about the same time a medical officer summed up what he saw as an average miner: 'At 40 or 45 he is a wheezing old man with a more or less barrel-shaped chest, coughing and spitting, incapable of much exertion, with more or less blueness of the lips and before 50 he is usually forced to give up work.' The shape of the chest could well have been influenced by a tendency to work hard and play hard – and the play could take the form of consuming vast quantities of strong drink in smoke-ridden alehouses where they were often paid.

Matters eventually led to the setting up in 1863 of the Kinnaird Commission to investigate the health and working conditions of miners. It found a much higher mortality rate through chest diseases than was the case with workers living in the more squalid parts of Liverpool. In Grassington the life expectancy of miners was 46 years compared with 56 years for those earning their livelihood by other means. Similar figures were prevalent elsewhere, although a surprising exception was Greenhow where miners working on the windswept heights were likely to live for another ten years. Most of the mines were in limestone, which did not create the same amounts of dust.

Typifying the approach of a time long before such basic precautions as face masks was the evidence of James Ray Eddy, the 6th Duke of Devonshire's chief mineral agent: 'In this district, I do not think that there is anything to damage the men's health, save boring in the gritstone; that is the bane of this country, and I believe that what I am trying to get them into at present, namely wearing a moustache, is the only preventative for it.'

The Kinnaird Commission did not bring radical changes. In one respect conditions got worse following the invention in 1866 of dynamite, which increased productivity and thus created even more toxic fumes. More fundamental was the fact that medical science was not yet sufficiently advanced to diagnose the risks from silicosis, caused by particles of fine mineral dust scarring the lungs and making miners more susceptible to tuberculosis. Not until 1882 did Robert Koch prove this dire condition to be an infectious disease, a breakthrough for which he subsequently received the Nobel Prize for Medicine. It came just too late to save the miners.

Religion

Despite a short life expectancy and all the grief it entailed, there was initially little in the way of spiritual comfort. By the late eighteenth century the Church of England had lost touch with the more remote parts of northern England. Great crowds gathered when John Wesley, the evangelist of nonconformity, travelled through the Dales. In his journal for 1768 he noted: 'I have not found so deep and lively a work in any other part of the Kingdom as runs through

Mining communities were responsible for building numerous Methodist chapels, one of the most impressive being at Gunnerside in Swaledale with seating for as many as 700. Sadly, by the time it was opened in 1867 the lead industry was already in decline, although today it is still beautifully maintained.

the whole circuit, particularly in the vales which wind through these horrid mountains.' The exuberance of Methodist teachings appealed to miners and their independent spirit, giving them hope and a determination to take control of their own lives. Most of them converted to the new faith preached by men of their own class in a language they could understand. It became commonplace to stop and say a prayer before entering a mine.

Vicars and curates of the Church of England were of the upper and middle classes, without the sympathy for their parishioners possessed by Methodist preachers. Matters were not helped by the necessity of many mining families to share a single home with the result that marriages were postponed and illegitimate children were frequent. Prejudice was epitomised by the Reverend Doctor Thomas Dunham Whitaker, a haughty cleric who combined the attributes of a scholarly historian with supreme bigotry. He unpleasantly stigmatised miners as 'colluvies' – a now archaic term for collections of filth or foul matter – who had contributed more to an increase of population than to the improvement of order and good morals.

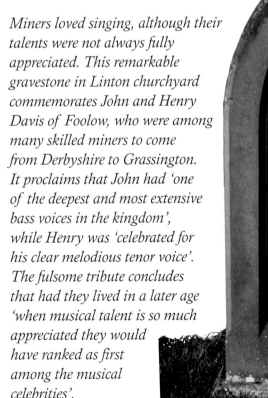

Miners loved singing, although their talents were not always fully appreciated. This remarkable gravestone in Linton churchyard commemorates John and Henry Davis of Foolow, who were among many skilled miners to come from Derbyshire to Grassington. It proclaims that John had 'one of the deepest and most extensive bass voices in the kingdom', while Henry was 'celebrated for his clear melodious tenor voice'. The fulsome tribute concludes that had they lived in a later age 'when musical talent is so much appreciated they would have ranked as first among the musical celebrities'.

Such attitudes merely increased the spread of Methodism in mining communities. Wesleyans soon eclipsed the predominance of the Established Church and from 1812 the breakaway and less sober Primitive Methodists proved to have even greater appeal. Their 'love feasts' were the equivalent of today's revivalist rallies. Few of the many converts heeded the doubts of a Wesleyan preacher over whether 'night meetings, particularly in the winter season, be for good or be for ill to the morals of young men and women, if unaccompanied by their parents and friends'.

The restraining influences of Methodism gradually changed the way of life. Preaching had at first taken place at cockfights, simply because here were to be found the greatest congregations of people, but sports and pastimes now became more civilised. Alcohol was seen as the root of all evil and the temperance movement gained in strength in the mid-19th century. Gatherings of Bands of Hope would begin with a procession of Sunday

Almost every mining community came to have a brass band. This early photograph dates from about 1870 when knowledge of spelling and the three Rs was still scant. The inscription on the drum reads 'Grassington Amature' and its members from left to right were; Jim Holmes, Sam Parker, Wilson Salkell, William Latham, Tom Ashton, William Gill, Fred Waddilove, Charlie Simpson, John Bake, James Simpson, John Brown and Mose Nelson, with Bob Simpson sitting in front. (Arthur Raistrick collection)

School children carrying 'respectable banners' to the accompaniment of a brass band playing the National Anthem. Those present would be served with medicinal water followed by a cold collation. Melodies would be played before speeches on the evils of alcohol and the need to sign the pledge. It all proved surprisingly effective with a decline in the number of pubs and the consumption of more tea and less ale.

Leisure and learning

Sundays were always sacred but on other days of the week the arduous life of a miner meant that the most was made of what little leisure time was available. Shortage of food drove many to be skilled poachers to the benefit of both their family's diet and their health. Hound trailing was especially popular as was fishing, perhaps because it centred on expectancy in a similar way to mining. More vigorous activities such as boxing and wrestling were once especially popular.

Apart from stronger religious beliefs, there was a growing move towards self-improvement. Miners recognised the need to have an elementary knowledge of arithmetic and a basic understanding of geology in order to secure the best terms under the complex bargaining system. They also had to be aware of the perils in handling gunpowder and later dynamite. Hence the growth in well-patronised literary institutes, libraries and reading rooms. Another change for the better was setting up Friendly Societies where money could be put aside to cover loss of earnings through sickness and the absolute certainty of funeral costs.

Most men had a hobby – anything from wood carving to knitting. Communal entertainment centred round agricultural and flower shows as well as fairs and feasts, when country dancing would last late into the night. A once great musical tradition in the Dales that is now virtually forgotten was passed down from generation to generation, with miners being especially noted for their singing. They took their instruments into chapel to accompany the hymns and psalms and were saddened when it became fashionable to install harmoniums or pipe organs. A new outlet for their talents was provided by forming brass bands, which came to be a feature of virtually every mining community.

Sad times

Music and singing would normally cheer the heart, or even a troubled mind, but it must have become increasingly difficult as the mining peak of the 1850s ebbed away. Those in the Dales with smallholdings would try to cling on to what little they possessed, but finding a farm to rent was difficult and then as now affordable land was at a premium. In the days long before subsidies, it was also unlikely to produce sufficient food and income for survival.

By the late 1880s many miners were earning as little as nine shillings [£45] per week and were close to starvation. They and their families were faced with no alternative to packing their meagre belongings and making a sad farewell. It was in many ways a re-run of events in the early 1830s, although this time it was on a more devastating and permanent scale. Men in Swaledale sought employment in the Durham coal mines, while those in the southern dales again fared better in the West Riding and Lancashire as their womenfolk could work in the textile mills. As previously, many also headed overseas to America. They all left behind a unique way of life in a remote world of close-knit mining communities. As related in the second part of the book, it was a remarkable legacy in key settlements in Swaledale as well as those such as Greenhow, Grassington and Hebden.

Several of these men working at Metcalf Mine, Illinois, in 1904 had emigrated from Swaledale. (David Morris collection, Swaledale Museum Archive)

PART 2

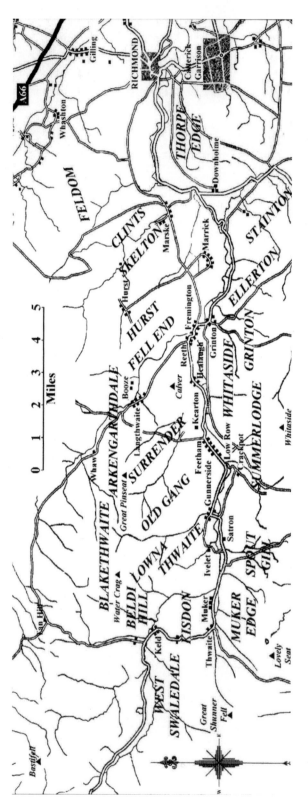

Swaledale, showing the location of villages covered in this chapter and also lead mines as instanced by Beldi Hill, Blakethwaite, Old Gang, Surrender, Arkengarthdale and Hurst. (M.C. Gill)

4. Swaledale

Swaledale and its tributary valley of Arkengarthdale formed by far the largest of all lead-mining areas in the Yorkshire Dales. Well over a thousand miners – almost a quarter of the total population – lived there at the industry's peak. It was a figure not remotely matched in other dales. Several individual villages had more miners than other key settlements such as Grassington and Hebden in Wharfedale, and collectively they played their part in enabling Swaledale to produce about half of Yorkshire's lead output.

The dramatic landscape has few equals. Swaledale is a deep west to east valley with most villages clinging to small areas of level land on its sunny north side. They often lie at the foot of tributary gills, which cut through the main veins of lead also running from west to east. At such points the ore was on or very close to the surface and thus was readily worked from the earliest times. It was also easily accessible by driving levels from the bottom of these gills into the hillside.

As the Norse place-names suggest, most of the villages are long established and would have developed even if lead had not been close at hand. Miners simply added to their size, with their numbers closely relating to the richness of the veins. The figures in the 1851 census at a peak of lead output include outlying hamlets and farms but give a good indication of the main mining settlements. Working downdale, Keld and Muker at its head had 133 miners and the totals then went higher in accord with the greater yields of lead. Gunnerside had 208 and there were 276 in the closely related villages of Low Row, Feetham and Healaugh.

This figure was slightly exceeded by the total of 284 in Arkle Town, Langthwaite and Booze in Arkengarthdale (always known locally as 'Arkendale'), whose position in a tributary valley set them apart. Even more on their own were the inhabitants of Hurst, over the hill to the east but still some 1,200ft above sea level. It had a modest 71 miners in 1851 but they formed a much higher proportion of the population than elsewhere as it was the only village created specifically to serve the mines.

Working downdale, this chapter looks in turn at the above settlements. One striking omission might appear to be Reeth, which is certainly grander

Gateway to the mines. By far the largest village in the dale, Reeth was always a supply and market centre rather than a settlement where miners lived in big numbers. This view captures a quiet moment in Silver Street about 1903. (Clive Torrens collection)

in scale than most Dales villages and owes much of this character to the wealth created by lead mining. Yet less than a tenth of the inhabitants of Swaledale's largest village were miners, several of these 60 men working at Grinton on the south side of the valley. Here lead deposits proved highly profitable to the first discoverers but their dreams of hidden wealth were not realised and output remained tiny compared with the north side of the dale. Reeth became an administrative and market centre where miners met but never dwelt in overwhelming numbers.

Keld and Muker

The upper reaches of Swaledale are divided by the distinctive green hill of Kisdon, which has Keld at its head and Muker at its foot. There have been small mines on Kisdon but their deposits and place in history were to be totally eclipsed when a rich vein was found a mile to the east of Keld above spectacular waterfalls in the river's limestone gorge. It played centre stage in what has winged down the ages as the 'Battle of Beldi Hill' and become one of the most infamous sagas in mining history. Its roots go way back to 1544 when Henry VIII, in return for support, granted the manor of Muker and a half share in that of Healaugh to Sir Thomas

Philip, 4th Lord Wharton 1613 - 1696, who controlled most mineral rights in Swaledale west of Reeth. He had the resources to play a pioneering role in the development of lead mining, as at the age of 12 he had inherited vast estates and an annual income of some £8,000 – the equivalent of over £1¼ million today. This portrait by Anthony van Dyck shows him at about the age of 19, when he was noted as 'one of the handsomest of men and the greatest beau of his times'. (Andrew Mellon Collection, National Gallery of Art, Washington D.C.)

Wharton. These manors extended far beyond the villages of the same name and ownership conferred control of the mineral rights over much of Swaledale west of Reeth. As the value of lead deposits came to be recognised, it must have seemed a promising investment to Philip, 4th Lord Wharton, when in 1635 he was able to acquire the other half of Healaugh for the precise sum of £3,173 7s 6d [a less precise £470,000].

All went well until the 5th Lord's son proved to be such an unstable spendthrift that he lost £20,000 [£2,800,000] in the South Sea Bubble of 1722 and his estate was placed in the hands of trustees. In 1738 they felt obliged to sell the two manors but retained mineral rights on the commons and waste lands. In the light of subsequent events it was a division that could have been more precisely defined.

The manors were bought by Thomas Smith, who overcame several competing bids to secure them for the considerable sum of £10,500 [£1,475,000]. A successful attorney at Gray's Inn in London, he was also a recluse who rarely ventured from his chambers and may well never have visited Swaledale. Where he owned the mineral rights on enclosed land, these were let to a series of entrepreneurs who searched for lead with often mixed results.

So it was that in May 1767 a group guided by John Parke of Low Row struck an especially rich vein on Beldi Hill, regarding their presence as legitimate because it was one of the intake pastures of Crackpot Hall Farm rather than common land. It happened at a time when mining rights on the outlying common had in 1764 passed by marriage to the 2nd Earl of Pomfret, a courtier and gambler with a great fondness for duelling. Charged at the Old Bailey with murder when he killed a British army captain during a duel with swords, he somehow managed to escape with a pardon. He was later said to be 'disordered in his mind' – a condition that has been ascribed to syphilis.

Hence trouble was virtually inevitable when the Earl decided that Beldi Hill fell within the common. He enlisted the services of William I'Anson, another noted attorney, who practised in Bedford Row, London, as well as in Leyburn. Accompanied by John Metcalfe, Pomfret's chief mine agent, I'Anson went in person to Beldi Hill in June 1769 to oversee the sinking of a shaft. A bottle of brandy was provided to toast health and success to Lord Pomfret with rousing cheers.

This was clearly too much for the miners who, under the direction of John Parke, had been successfully extracting highly profitable amounts of ore for more than two years. Next morning they retaliated with a vengeance, when what was claimed to be 400 men led by Parke arrived on the Hill with the intention of filling in the Pomfret shaft. There followed a full-scale riot apparently lasting six hours with three men being pulled from this shaft 'by the hair of their heads' and thrown into a 27ft deep hush gutter. William I'Anson met the same fate by the use of 'great force and violence' along with three more miners.

Further disturbances continued throughout 1769. A local agent working for Parke ordered one of Pomfret's men out of his mine 'otherwise he should very likely break his shins'. Several attempts were later made to flood shafts that had been sunk by Parke's miners, and mutual recriminations continued to affect the property of both parties in a much wider area of Swaledale. Thomas Smith, as manorial owner and noted attorney, may have felt he was in a good position to obtain an injunction against Pomfret. Yet the judgment left a sense of the divine right of peers, as the Master of the Rolls refused to believe that his lordship was 'capable of working the mines by force in so illegal a manner',

Matters then moved up the legal scale with a two-day trial at York Assizes in August 1770. It was a ruinously expensive exercise with the inhabitants of Richmond no doubt gasping when a procession of six post-chaises and numerous horses carried over a hundred of Pomfret's witnesses through

At its height the Beldi Hill dispute attracted what today would be termed mass media coverage, including this fascinating cartoon published in the Oxford Magazine *in 1771. The 2nd Earl of Pomfret is the central figure, proclaiming: 'I'll turn all this lead to gold.' At right is his adversary Thomas Smith, protesting: 'If I lose my cause I must appeal to Heaven, which is the Highest Court of Justice, and his Lordship cannot follow me there.' (Lewis Walpole Library, Yale University)*

the town on their way to court. It was necessary for the jury to travel to Beldi Hill, described as 'a very high and wild mountain, in great part consisting of bogs, mosses and swangs [swamps] generally inaccessible at all times of the year but in the summer season'.

Pomfret was outraged when the verdict went in favour of Smith. He appeared in person on the steps of Richmond market cross and delivered a speech described by one local inhabitant as 'foolish, artful, stupid, designing, dull and mad'. According to local press reports he threatened the jury with prison for giving a false verdict and there is evidence the he challenged one of the jurors to a duel. He went on to lodge an appeal in the House of Lords and won by 17 votes to 10.

Thomas Smith was not to be defeated and a second jury trial took place before the Court of King's Bench, Westminster in November 1772. Alexander Wadderburn, the Solicitor General, presented what has been described as a masterly argument – and this time the verdict went in Smith's favour. When the news reached Swaledale there was great celebration with bonfires lit, bells rung and ox roasted.

Smith died in January 1773 at the age of 80 just weeks after the final verdict, although a Rev Thomas Smith was still Lord of the Manor until 1868. Pomfret was left so much in debt that he immediately had to sell Sunbury Court, the magnificent house in Middlesex he had inherited through marriage. Imprisoned in the Tower of London in 1780 following a dispute with the Duke of Grafton, he died five years later. Pomfret never paid his miners and his chief mine agent was declared bankrupt. Nor did he meet the fees of his attorney, William I'Anson, who wrote to a fellow lawyer that he had been cheated out of a bill of almost £1,500 [£170,000] and even considered getting away from it all by finding a post in the East Indies. At least his daughter was destined to achieve musical immortality. I'Anson had married Martha Hutchinson of Hill House, Richmond, and Frances born in 1766 was the romantic heroine in the famous song *Sweet Lass of Richmond Hill.*

As for Beldi Hill, the mine was greatly expanded and continued to operate for more than a century. In 1846 it saw one of the last instances of hushing in Swaledale, when a group of 20 miners was led by James

Beldi Hill – scene of battle. In the foreground are the remains of the mine's crushing mill and beyond is the crumbling Crackpot Hall, declared unfit for human habitation in 1953.

Kearton. He was landlord in Muker of the Miners' Arms, the name also adopted by the pub at Keld which previously and then later was the more memorable Cat Hole Inn. The group reverted to the time-honoured practice of building dams to expose lead by releasing a sudden flush of water. Close to Crackpot Hall Farm, these were watched night and day by two men and the venture proved so successful that it lasted for another 16 years. The damage that hushing inflicted on rivers was a reason why it fell out of favour and it cannot have helped the land immediately around the farmhouse, which in any event became a casualty of mining operations. There is a certain irony that the setting for so much former trouble was in 1953 declared unfit for human habitation owing to subsidence and subsequently fell into ruin.

A great handicap in mining at Beldi Hill was the utter and overwhelming inaccessibility of upper Swaledale. The nearest small town of Hawes was seven miles away and involved a perilous climb with a yawning gap on one side before reaching the 1,700ft summit of Buttertubs Pass. A rough track led west from Keld to Kirkby Stephen in Westmorland but both routes had severe limitations. There was often no alternative to the 18-mile journey down the valley from Muker to Richmond, which even today is not for those in a hurry.

Muker was long a self-sufficient community with a weekly market where miners and farmers met to buy food and fare. Essential supplies would often be lacking in the winter months, as for example when baking was impossible because snow prevented the brewery carter bringing yeast from Kirkby Stephen. With or without such vital ingredients, all present would adjourn to one of the three pubs and frequently had to rely on their horses to find the way home. These hostelries were always open day and night for the four-day festival of Muker Awd Roy, beginning on Twelfth Night in January and thus probably a survival of the ancient Epiphany Feast. All work in the mines was suspended and there was dancing from dusk to dawn. Fighting was also commonplace, sometimes over disputes between miners but often as pre-arranged bare-fisted boxing contests.

The overcrowding that affected many mining communities in the early 19th century seems to have been especially serious in Muker. Cottages and farmhouses were converted into two or more 'livings', with bad sanitary conditions leading to deaths from smallpox and typhus. The opinionated Thomas Dunham Whitaker, who in 1805 castigated Grassington miners in his *History of Craven*, returned to the theme with a vengeance in his *History of Richmondshire,* posthumously published in 1823 and more noted for its illustrations by Turner than the quality of its research. Deploring

Muker about 1890, when memories of mining days could still be recalled but there was little life in the village. (Clive Torrens collection)

the way that Swaledale miners were polluting the river to the detriment of spawning fish, he condemned them as possessing 'a degree of ferocity very formidable when highly excited' and then roundly continued: 'In the mining villages are to be found those appearances of squalid neglect about the persons of the inhabitants, and those external accumulations of domestic filth about their dwellings.'

Any truth in Whitaker's allegations was overtaken by events. Owing to its isolation, Muker proved to be especially susceptible to downturns in mining with considerable emigration to America around 1830. Hopes of building a Methodist chapel were long delayed and did mot come to fruition until 1845, the cost being kept down to £96 [£8,500] by 36 members contributing their labour free. Such was the poverty of local miners that 344 of the 470 subscribers gave less than 2s 6d [£11].

A further quarter of the population was lost in the ten years to 1861 and today it seems inconceivable that the village once suffered from overcrowding. Jocelyn M. Campbell, writing a preface in 2010 to a new edition of Edmund Cooper's classic history of Muker, noted the closure of its school, chapel, shops and post office. She concluded with mixed feelings:

'Not only have outlying farms become second or retiral homes, but even in the village the local families, who have lived there for generations, find themselves

*living next door to houses occupied for only a few weeks each year. A way
of life which had remained relatively unchanged for centuries has altered
dramatically, perhaps for the worse, but hopefully for the better.'*

Gunnerside

The village of Gunnerside is at the foot of one of the most spectacular
of all lead-mining valleys, only three miles long but 500 feet deep from
moor top to beck bottom. The narrow confines of Gunnerside Gill display
hushing on a grand scale, mine workings perched on the hillside, the only
deep level in Swaledale and ruined buildings in remote locations that were
once thatched dwellings scantily housing large families.

It all owes much to the successors of the infamous 2nd Earl of Pomfret.
Prior to him inheriting the mineral rights on the commons and waste
lands of most of the north side of Swaledale by marriage in 1764, they
had been administered by the Wharton trustees with Alexander Denton
at their head. It is probable that his initials thereafter led to the collective
name A.D. Mines. On the death of the 2nd Earl in 1785 they passed
to his three children, who were all minors. His daughter Lady Charlotte
married Peter Denys, a dancing master who might have seemed the last
person to shape future mining policy. Yet he became closely interested
during frequent visits to Swaledale but felt there was no suitable local
inn in which to stay. The problem was solved in 1792 by purchasing a
house in Fremington, near Reeth, which was enlarged and named A.D.
Hall. Appropriately enough a lead statue of Saturnus was placed in the
grounds of the property, which was later re-named Draycott Hall after
Anna Maria Draycott, wife of the 2nd Earl.

In many ways Peter Denys made the right decisions, as in an era when
ever greater investment was needed he opted to minimise risks by splitting
mining areas into large blocks that were leased to venture capitalists.
Gunnerside Gill marked the boundary between two blocks with the west
side comprising Lownathwaite and Blakethwaite mines, which had a
series of lessees. The east side was the edge of a much larger and richer
area extending two miles eastwards to the far side of Barney Beck. Its
name – Old Gang – seems highly fitting for the rough and tumble of
mining but in fact 'Gang' simply relates to strong veins of lead.

In 1811 this block was leased to George and Thomas Alderson, London
lead merchants, who as absentees relied on an agent. John Davies proved
to be a flawed choice and was perhaps overawed by the sheer size of Old
Gang. Within three years expenditure had exceeded receipts by £20,000
[£1¼ million] resulting in his dismissal. There was no sustained surge

Draycott Hall, Fremington, named after Anna Maria Draycott, wife of the 2nd Earl of Pomfret. Her daughter married Peter Denys, who bought the property in 1792 as a base for administering the A.D. Mines stretching over most of the north side of Swaledale.

forward until 1828 when the lease passed to a company comprised entirely of local men. Jaques & Co had already achieved considerable success in Arkengarthdale and was to transform the fortunes of Old Gang. Robert Jaques was from a family that had made its wealth in the East India Company and had a large estate at Easby, near Richmond.

It was as well there were sufficient reserves and local determination to see Gunnerside through the recession that hit the village especially hard. In 1827 it was a thriving community with 117 Wesleyan members attending its chapel, which had been built in 1789 at a cost of £600 [£66,000]. Methodism in Swaledale had gained strength following at least three visits by John Wesley and a visiting preacher to the Reeth District later noted that 'crowds of miners came pouring down the craggy hills' to worship. The musical tradition was fostered with an especially warm welcome being given to evangelist minister Hodgson Casson, who was felt to be something of an eccentric but a good singer.

Yet in a mere seven years through to 1834 the number of Wesleyans in Gunnerside had declined to a mere 34. Richard Garth, living on the south side of the valley, noted in his 1830 day book: 'The very low price of lead has reduced wages to a starving state – great numbers with their families gone off – and pauperism has become almost general.' His near neighbour Edward Broderick referred to friends who had packed their bundles of bedding and provisions into carts before embarking on the long journey over to Liverpool and then across the Atlantic by sailing ship to start a new life.

Notable among them was miner James Pratt, who emigrated with his wife Hannah in 1833. After they had first cleared land for a farm in Ohio, he walked 500 miles in 17 days and helped to found a new lead-mining centre at Dubuque on the west bank of the Mississippi in Iowa. By the time he died in 1869 he was a prosperous mill-owner regarded as 'one of the noblest' of all settlers.

Back in Gunnerside the hard times continued into the late 1830s. Unemployed miners who stayed at home were provided with work in 1835 by building a new bridge across the Swale, one of them reputedly shedding tears when he saw a bottle of brandy about to be walled into the south pier for luck. Tradition inevitably relates that he was first allowed a sip! The bridge came to be criticised for its 'somewhat uneven appearance', which may have been due to flood damage as much as the use of an unskilled labour force.

New bridge across the Swale at Gunnerside, built by unemployed miners in 1835 as a job creation scheme. It superseded the 17th century Ivelet bridge, which still survives with its graceful single span.

Those who stuck it out ultimately saw a revival in both mining and Methodist worship. It was an age when most adults attended chapel twice on Sundays and from the 1851 religious census it has been calculated that the numbers at Gunnerside were 70 in the morning, 287 in the afternoon and 135 in the evening. The village was now the focal point of Methodism in Swaledale with a crowning moment coming in 1867 with the building of an imposing new chapel in Italianate style seating 700 and costing £800 [£63,000].

Yet doubts were already appearing on the mining front as most accessible ore in the Gill had been extracted. It was a situation grasped by Sir George Denys, grandson of Peter Denys, who decided to play an active role in driving a deep level starting 1¼ miles north of Gunnerside village on the west side of the Gill. Following the boundary separating Lownathwaite and Blakethwaite mines from Old Gang, the project involved first intercepting and then draining the main veins almost a mile distant at the valley head and some 200 feet below the surface. Sir George named the new venture Sir Francis Level after his son and heir in expectation that it would unlock new reserves and provide 'a feast of fat things for generations to come'.

Work started in 1864 but like all such operations it was a slow task. At first the level advanced by nearly seven feet per week using hand-bored shotholes and black powder blasting but after three years this figure fell to less than three feet. By 1869 only 400 yards had been completed by four men working in pairs for two six-hour shifts daily.

Sir George calculated that at this rate of progress it would take another 25 years to reach the main vein. He concluded that compressed-air boring would have to be introduced 'to bring the science of the 19th century to the aid of our jog-trot notions'. The company in charge of the work declined and so he took it over himself, providing a waterwheel-driven compressor in an engine house at the entrance to the level. It was the first use of such technology in Yorkshire. The equipment was suitably maintained by John Calvert, one of five blacksmiths once active in Gunnerside, and progress was further accelerated with the introduction of dynamite in 1873. It was an ebullient moment when ore was cut four years later after a mile of tunneling, the work so far having cost over £6,000 [£500,000] with explosives alone amounting to £600 [£50,000].

The second stage of the project was to enable the search for ore to go a further 130 feet deep by building an underground chamber at the inner end of the level to house a hydraulic winding engine. This would be capable of pumping 500 gallons of water a minute and lifting 24 tons of ore per hour. There was great ceremony when the work was completed in September 1880 to the delight of Sir George: 'We had a festival at Sir Francis to commemorate the event. Speeches, songs, band of music, 30 gallons of beer and miners all very happy.' The overall cost of the engine and associated works was £4,500 [£400,000] and sadly it was a venture that came just too late. Sir George died in February 1881 and never saw his scheme in operation. The engine was started in July of that year, but lack of ore in the lower beds coupled with the continuing dire price of lead made it uneconomic to continue and they were stopped the following summer.

In summer 1879 the diarist John Henry Wilkinson visited Gunnerside and in the then William IV Inn met the part owner of Blakethwaite Mine. Blaming the flood of cheap lead from abroad, he described the amount of ore being extracted as 'pitiful'. He had had to lay off workers and feared for their future as there was precious little other employment in the dale. The concerns voiced in the inn proved to be an accurate prediction. Lead mining in the Gill continued on a minor scale for the rest of the 19th century but never regained its former levels and finally stopped in 1906. It took a long time for Gunnerside to recover. Writing her pioneer work on Swaledale in 1934, Ella Pontefract noted: 'Situated as it was in the very heart of the mining district, it suffered perhaps more than other villages at their closing down, and showed it in its look of ruin and desolation.'

Low Row, Feetham and Healaugh
The villages of Swaledale are not separated by great distances. Low Row – locally known as 'Lah Rah' – is less than two miles from Gunnerside and took its name from a straggling row of houses set below the road through the settlement. Such dwellings became a feature of the dale when miners built onto existing farmhouses. The village merges with Feetham, which like Keld and Muker once adopted the Miners' Arms name for its pub. Two miles further east is Healaugh, which typified the height of the mining era in 1851 with a population of 251 occupying just 46 houses. They included 48 miners, two lead carriers, two lead agents and, most striking of all, 112 children under the age of 15. Some homes had 12 occupants and only one bedroom.

All three villages were some three miles from the rich eastern edge of Old Gang mining field close to the upper reaches of Barney Beck, which joined the River Swale near Healaugh. It was a then tolerable walk to work, although a harder challenge had to be met by miners from Gunnerside who joined them. They were faced with either a climb of almost a thousand feet on a direct route or a detour up Gunnerside Gill and then over the lowest point of Melbecks Moor.

The present-day scene inside Hard Level, one of the most successful of all the Old Gang mines. It ultimately formed part of an extraordinary underground chain of levels stretching for four miles from Gunnerside Gill to Arkengarthdale. (courtesy David Harper and Paul Steggles, Swaledale Museum Archive)

Opposite, top: *Hand-knitting was for many centuries a major activity in the northern dales. Especially popular with miners were long and thick stockings on which they could kneel. George Walker depicted hand-knitting in Wensleydale in his classic 1814 book* The Costume of Yorkshire, *but sadly he did not include lead miners among the 40 occupations that he portrayed in colour.*

Lower: *Paradise, the large house in Low Row that was originally a two-storey building. A top storey was added in the 18th century after it had become a centre for hand-spinning. It long provided employment for the dependents of miners until it proved impossible to compete with factory looms in the urban mill towns. (Clive Torrens collection)*

A small community thus grew up near the headwaters of Barney Beck, known at this point as Hard Level Gill, where miners could lodge in buildings centred on Level House and bring with them enough food to last from Monday until Saturday. Bedsteads would accommodate three or four men and comprised large wooden frames with an under-mattress of rope mesh netting, on top of which was a further straw or chaff mattress. Like

the mining on either side of the Gill, these arrangements were established at an early date. In 1692 Ann Barker of Level House died and was buried in linen at a time when only wool was permitted. Accused of failing to help the wool trade, her father Adam was commanded by the local High Sheriff to levy the hefty sum of £5 [£700] from her goods and chattels. In what is thought to be the last recorded case of its kind in England, half of this sum was to be distributed to the poor and the remainder to an informant who had no doubt seen a ready source of financial gain.

The Hard Level name had already been given to what became one of the most successful Old Gang mines with a complex network of veins producing highly profitable ore throughout the 1790s and the first ten years of the 19th century. The ore was taken to smelt mills lower down the valley, with the most famous and ultimately the largest Old Gang Mill just a mile distant having four ore hearths and a slag hearth. The peat house, almost 400 feet long, could store a year's supply of fuel cut by a team of over 20 men, which was sometimes augmented by coal from King's Pit near Tan Hill. Other buildings included a joiner's shop, stables, powder store and offices with a pay room being provided in 1843. This was presumably in response to recent legislation, outlawing the previous practice whereby money had been paid to miners in the Feetham pub on the third Thursday of the month only for much of it to be promptly spent on strong liquor.

Female and child labour was still prevalent, as reflected in the 1851 census for Low Row which was especially detailed in listing occupations. Four of the six lead ore dressers were female and so too were three of the six inhabitants who described themselves as lead ore washers. The remaining three were boys aged only 11 and 12, although no doubt they had a better working life than the nine-year old 'lead mine machine blower' who would spend many hours in darkness turning the handle of the 'Windy King' fan in an attempt to improve ventilation underground.

These were productive years at Old Gang with output of lead recorded at 2,097 tons in 1857 and valued at £27,266 [£2¼ million] three years later. In 1862 there were 229 miners but production was then falling, only to recover with the mine making an average annual profit of over £4,000 [£375,000] in the years from 1867 to 1872. Only in the late 1870s did it follow the general pattern of going into a long and steady decline, culminating in closure in 1887 followed by unsuccessful attempts at revival.

There was a similar trend in a much smaller mining field beyond Old Gang on the north-east side of Barney Beck. Working downdale it was the last part of Healaugh Manor owned in the late 17th century by the

Lords Wharton and led up to the boundary with Arkengarthdale Manor then owned by the Bathurst family. The division between the two was ill defined and when lead was found in this area a dispute was predictable. In 1699 Wharton's miners filled in a shaft in which Bathurst's men were working and nearly killed them. A three-year case in the Court of Chancery was followed by a trial ordered by the House of Lords.

The outcome was inconclusive and the matter rumbled on for almost another century. It was inflamed in 1778 by the quarrelsome 2nd Earl of Pomfret, who was still not entirely subdued by the outcome of the Beldi Hill verdict six years earlier. His men sunk shafts that were filled in by Arkengarthdale miners amid much violence on both sides. Not until 1797 did an agreement resolve that the disputed ground was part of Healaugh Manor, and it must have been salt in the wound to Arkengarthdale interests when it was given the name Surrender Mine. It proved very rich, producing over a thousand tons of lead in 1801 and having its own smelt mill close to Barney Beck under a new lease made in 1839. The surge in output seen at Old Gang in the late 1860s was not matched at Surrender and both mine and mill closed in 1880.

Miners from Low Row, Feetham and Healaugh working at Old Gang and Surrender saw a massive change in their way of life as soon as decline took hold in the mid-1870s. Hard times for their families were compounded by the swift-flowing River Swale and its tributaries being far from ideal for textile mills. There was thus no ready employment for women and children on the same scale as in the mining communities of Grassington and Hebden in Upper Wharfedale. There was hope unfulfilled of falling back on the hand-knitting of stockings, which locally dated back to Tudor times when this type of legwear had replaced the hose as preferred garments. With both vagueness and precision, a 1595 government survey noted: 'About one thousand families do make about 166 dozen long stockings every week in about 20 villages around Richmond.'

Groups of women gathered to gossip and sing as well as knit long stockings that were always in demand by miners. Often they took it in turns to have knitting nights in each other's houses so as to save candlelight and fire. There is a long-held tradition that menfolk also indulged as they tramped across the moor on their way to work, although the prospect of a muscular miner using needles instead of a pickaxe is difficult to visualise.

Low Row and Feetham were centres of hand-knitting, largely because wool could be obtained in Paradise. This was no heavenly delight but rather the name of a large house in Low Row that has come to be considered a monument of outstanding national significance. A rare survival of the transitional period between people working in their own homes and being employed in factories, it accommodated hand-powered devices for spinning wool for knitting. The machinery was owned not by the workers but by the employer, who lived under the same roof. The latterday owners were the Knowles family, who also had a fulling mill at Haverdale on the opposite side of the valley where garments knitted in unwashed wool were cleaned and shrunk in soapy water before being sold. Sadly, these enterprises could not compete with the age of factory looms and succumbed in 1870 just ahead of the decline of mining at Old Gang and Surrender. As proved to be the case in Gunnerside, this part of Swaledale was left with little else.

Arkengarthdale
Arkle Town, Langthwaite and Booze

These three small settlements clustered close together in Arkengarthdale offered miners one great advantage compared with those in the rest of Swaledale. There was no lengthy tramp to work, as the main veins cutting though the higher reaches of Gunnerside and Hard Level Gills was here closer to hand. Mining extended over more than 800 years and its scars are more visible than elsewhere. Hushes cut into both sides of the valley and there are spoil heaps in profusion. Those who grieve their presence ought instead to lament the loss of the magnificent Octagon Smelt Mill, surviving until its demolition 70 years ago, which today would have been one of the most outstanding buildings in the Yorkshire Dales.

Arkengarthdale Manor was bought in 1656 by John Bathurst of Blackfriars in London, who was Oliver Cromwell's 'Doctor of Phiseike' and twice M.P. for Richmond. He founded a grammar school in the dale for his tenants, almost all of whom were illiterate, and gave widows a shilling each quarter if they regularly went to church. It was then a different settlement pattern, as shown in 1676 with just five tenants in the valley bottom at Arkle Town and Langthwaite. The majority – eleven in number – were high on the hillside at Booze. Its enticing name has nothing to do with thirsty miners but means the house by the bow or curve, reflecting its position overlooking Arkle Beck. It may just be a coincidence that the local pronunciation of 'bouse' – the material emerging from a mine – would probably have been close to 'booze'.

The manor passed in turn to three descendants, each with the forename Charles. The third Charles Bathurst moved in high circles, also becoming M.P. for Richmond as well as Northern Grandmaster of the Freemasons in 1726 and then High Sheriff of Yorkshire the following year. A complex

The initials of Charles Bathurst came to be given to the C.B. Mines in Arkengarthdale. They are still remembered by the C.B. Inn north of Langthwaite, seen here about 1910. (Clive Torrens collection)

character, he reputedly looked after his miners' love of smoking clay pipes by sending them tobacco from London. A touch unstable, he was in more of a spot of bother when he killed his butler with a sword during a drunken brawl. There were large debts when he died childless in 1743. Out of the three Charles Bathursts he was probably the one who led to the C.B. initials being adopted for the Arkengarthdale mines. It was convenient brevity, as it meant ownership of most mines on the north side of Swaledale could simply be referred to as either A.D. or C.B. Today the same initials are still remembered in the name of the C.B. Inn north of Langthwaite.

Annual profits from the mines had been valued at £3,000 [£428,000] in 1731. Development should have been helped following easier contact with the outside world when in 1770 the apology for a road running from east of Brough past Tan Hill and down Arkengarthdale to Reeth became a turnpike. Yet by the 1790s the mines were regarded as 'very poor'. As had happened elsewhere, most of the readily accessible ore had been extracted and absentee landlords did not have the capital to finance exploitation of deeper deposits. After considerable disagreement it was decided to lease operations to an established company that could adopt modern methods of mining. Hence an agreement was signed in 1801 with Easterby, Hall & Co, lead merchants of Stockton-on-Tees.

Its partners had invaluable contacts in Stockton with Matthew Wadeson, the shipping agent responsible for the sale and dispatch of lead. His role was crucial as mines in the northern Dales were now at a disadvantage compared with those to the south. Grassington was only 10 miles from water-borne transport at Skipton following completion in 1777 of the eastern end of the Leeds & Liverpool Canal but it was a journey well over three times this distance from Arkengarthdale to the highest navigable reaches of the Tees at Stockton. Here Peter Denys of the A.D. Mines built a wharf from where Wadeson arranged dispatch in sailing ships, mostly to London but also to Hull and Newcastle as well as Dutch and German ports and occasionally via the Baltic to St Petersburg and Memel in Lithuania.

Only gradually did the problems of getting lead out of the dale ease, first with improvement in 1810 of navigation on the Tees and then on the first stage of the journey by building a turnpike road from Reeth to Richmond in 1836. Finally, ten years later Richmond was linked to the rapidly developing railway network which cut the cost of transporting lead to Stockton by about a third.

The dominant partner in Easterby, Hall & Co was Frederick Hall, who moved into Scar House in Langthwaite and was regarded as a dynamic figure with 'some reverse traits'. Charles Fothergill, a Wensleydale Quaker visiting the area in 1805, noted in his diary: 'Mr Hall deserves the highest credit, tho' many find fault with him as agent because he will do everything in the most superior style and is consequently very expensive to his employers; it seems he has been accustomed to the mining business in various parts of northern Europe.'

Fothergill also visited what Hall must have seen as a crowning achievement. Existing smelt mills in the dale were old and incapable of increased output, and so ground was cleared for the massive Octagon Mill close to the start of the Stang road from Langthwaite to Barnard Castle. Completed in 1804, it was 107ft long by 70ft wide and housed a 36ft diameter waterwheel powering the blowing machinery for six ore hearths. The Quaker diarist noted that it was 'one of the largest buildings in Europe under one roof' and perhaps optimistically claimed it was capable of smelting lead to the value of £3,600 [£270,000] per week.

Hall decided to increase his labour force by paying miners weekly instead of every six months as had previously been the practice. The population of the dale rose from 1,186 in 1801 to a peak of 1,529 ten years later, the influx of strangers from Durham, Northumberland, Cumberland and Westmorland having a noticeable effect on the local dialect with the loss of 'many expressions and comprehensive words'. Changes were reflected in the village communities, with increased numbers at Arkle Town Methodist chapel opened in 1798. It originally had the Anglican church as its neighbour but its foundations were undermined by Arkle Beck and it was replaced by a new structure at Langthwaite in 1818.

Many of the miners who moved into the dale had no smallholdings as an alternative source of income and soon proved to be hit especially hard. Easterby, Hall & Co had mortgaged its land to raise £3,000 [£217,000] towards development costs and was in trouble when their bank failed. Two partners were declared bankrupt and the company finally broke up in 1811. Frederick Hall went to work at Old Gang, only to be dismissed seven years later by the lessees George and Thomas Alderson whom he sued for damages of £60,000 [£4 million].

Hope returned to Arkengarthdale in 1821 when the mines were leased to Jaques & Co. It must have caused great delight to see affairs guided by local men rather than a company based at Stockton, which must then have been seen as on a distant foreign shore. Robert Jaques bought a property near the mines so that he had somewhere to stay when visiting them,

The magnificent Octagon Mill, completed in 1804 to house six ore hearths and demolished in 1944. If only it had survived a little longer it would surely have been revered as an outstanding example of industrial architecture. (Swaledale Museum Archive)

Scar House, Langthwaite, rebuilt in 1847 by the Rev John Gilpin who had inherited a share of the Arkengarthdale Mines through marriage. The moor beyond the woodland shows telltale signs of extensive opencast working and hushing, which has scarred much of this dale. It can either be viewed as desecration of once glorious scenery or wild industrial landscape at its finest!

as did another major investor, the Richmond solicitor Ottiwell Tomlin. The other partners were William Close, a former mayor or Richmond; Mathew Whitelock of Cogden Hall, Grinton; John Birkbeck of Low Row; and Edmund Knowles, owner of Haverdale Mill which played such a key role in Swaledale hand-knitting.

With their intimate knowledge of the mining field, they and their successors proved capable of guiding its fortunes for almost the next half century. They held fortnightly site meetings, closely supervising their agents and making a point of visiting the mines. An immediate and surprising decision was made to replace the Octagon Mill, which like its builders may have been over-ambitious. The New or C.B. Mill was built on land which the company owned and probably smelted its first lead in 1822. After a working life of just 18 years the Octagon Mill was henceforth placed on a care-and-maintenance basis. It did well to last until 1944.

Jaques & Co was soon employing 130 experienced miners, several of whom lived in purpose-built housing at C.B. Yard, close to the new mill, where a sawmill, stores and stables were also provided. By the late 1820s it was said that not a house was empty and the 1831 census recorded 285 men working in the lead industry. Development continued apace and the company kept up its efforts through the recession in lead prices of the late 1820s and early '30s. By 1841 there were 26 major levels, one of which formed the last link in an extraordinary four-mile underground chain that had no equal in the Dales. From the east side of Gunnerside Gill it was possible to enter Sir George Level, from where there was access to Bunting and Hard Levels. The next stage was a connection with the wonderfully named Brandy Bottle Incline, from where a side passage led into Surrender Mine. The final link would once have been unthinkable as it extended from Healaugh Manor into Arkengarthdale Manor before emerging into daylight at Moulds Level. It must have helped that Robert Jaques was also a partner at Surrender, although there continued to be differences between the manorial owners.

The west slopes of Arkengarthdale came to feature the wildest and most impressive mining landscape in northern England with a maze of opencast working and huge hushes. Their general name of the Hungry Hushes suggests that some did not provide the rich rewards expected. On the east side of the dale most of the mines were either in Slei Gill or above Booze. This remote community was a stronghold of Primitive Methodism by the mid-1820s but may have been living up to the implications of its name with alcohol not totally absent. In 1851 the population included 48 miners and the 41 houses reputedly had three selling beer and one with an illicit cockpit. The religious census in the same year showed that a hundred Primitive Methodists were attending the chapel at Langthwaite built in 1839, although it had to be mortgaged to pay off debts when their numbers rapidly declined in the mid-1850s.

These were good years for the mineral lords, even though the affairs of the manor had become increasingly complex. The last link with the Bathurst family was broken in 1808 when George Brown, a London banker, acquired a one-third share. He and his heirs gradually consolidated this position and they came to include the Rev John Gilpin, who in 1847 rebuilt Scar House as an impressive residence. The architect may have been John Dobson, far more celebrated as the creator of Newcastle station.

Unfortunately, by the late 1860s the long reign by Jaques & Co was losing its grip and had not long to live. The Arkengarthdale Mining Company was formed in 1870 with partners coming from as far afield as Magdelen College in Oxford and Northamptonshire. It took a hard line and sued the former lessees for almost £35,000 [£2¾ million] to restore the mines following alleged neglect and mismanagement.

Last gasp of lead mining in Arkengarthdale at Nut Hole Mine, Faggergill, briefly reopened in 1908. The two miners standing are Ashton Stones and Pratt Demain, and then from left to right are Ralph Harker, John Hird, George Harker (manager, in the tub wagon), Jimmy Waller, W. Longstaff, Ben Hall, Jack Alsop and Robert Langstaff, with George Hird in front. (James Backhouse, per M.C. Gill)

More seriously for the miners, it introduced new rules that forced the men to work six days a week with a six-hour shift beginning at 7.0am rather than an unspecified time. This was seen as an attack on their independence and the long-held custom of being a smallholder as well as a miner. It was a very rare event in December 1870 when the men went on strike. They held out for eight weeks until forced by starvation to return on their employers' terms, but bitterness long lingered and some 50 men reputedly left the dale rather than accept such an imposition.

The new company no doubt made much of the fact that it maintained a high level of output at a time when other mines in Swaledale were closing. Following valuable new discoveries this reached a peak of 1,967 tons in 1878. As late as the year to 30th June 1887 a profit of £5,243 [£520,700] was made on an output of over 1,400 tons.

Arkengarthdale was again lively, especially in its four beer houses and the five inns with such splendid names as the Jolly Dogs at Arkle Town and the Lily Jock at Langthwaite, which once reputedly had Sir Walter Scott as a guest. Attached to it was a room used as a miners' club where on special occasions the men wore off-white fustian trousers, coats with a tail known as a claw-hammer and cravats in which they fastened Lily Jock pins. The Mechanics' Institute at C.B. Terrace was also much used by miners.

Only in the 1890s did decline come to both Arkle Town and Langthwaite, while Booze was soon virtually deserted with more ruined houses than occupied dwellings. In just ten years the population of Arkengarthdale fell from 761 in 1891 to 427. Small-scale mining operations finally petered out in 1914 bringing to an end at least eight centuries of lead mining in the dale.

Hurst

It was once believed that a temple in Jerusalem was covered in lead brought by the Romans after it had been mined by slave labour at Hurst. What by a long way would have been the earliest mining in Swaledale was cited by Harry Speight in his 1897 book *Romantic Richmondshire*. He referred to the discovery at Hurst of a pig of lead stamped with the name of Emperor Adrian (117 - 138 AD) and claimed it was in the British Museum, but no subsequent trace of it has ever been found. It may be that this reference lived up to the 'romantic' part of the book's title and gave birth to legends culminating in the unlikely movement of lead out to the Middle East.

Over a thousand years elapsed before documentary evidence appears in relation to Marrick Priory, close to the River Swale east of Reeth and founded in the 12th century for Benedictine nuns. Delightful phraseology refers to lead for the roof coming from local mines that had been worked since 'time out of mind', some of which were centred on Hurst three miles to the north-west but 700 feet higher close to the moor top.

For the next 400 years the Manor of Marrick was owned by the successors of Roger Aske, closely associated with Richmond Castle. In 1535 it was inherited by Sir Ralph Bulmer and then passed to his son-in-law John Sayer, heralding a long period of lasting tension as they were both Catholics. On the dissolution of the monasteries, one of the Crown commissioners was John Uvedale who used his position to obtain Marrick Priory and its land. In 1580 his Protestant son Avery went direct to Queen Elizabeth regarding Sayer, alleging that he had incited 20 local men to take ore from his property 'with great force and avarice and in riotous manner and in strong hand, with staves, daggers, iron pikes and pyccals and other defensible weapons'.

Fines levied on recusants through much of the 17th century led to increasing debt and in 1648 control of the mines passed to Thomas Swinburne, a relative by marriage of the Bulmer family. About 1660 he built High Smelt Mill, close to Ellers Beck a mile north of Marrick village, which today is considered to be the best-preserved 17th century lead smelting mill in Britain and possibly the world.

Swinburne employed some 20 miners but did not prosper and in a 32-month period it cost him £2,559 [£367,000] to produce lead to the value of £2,678 [£384,000]. Such miniscule profit led to the mines being sold in 1668 to Charles Powlett, son of the Marquis of Winchester, who confessed that he preserved his estates by feigning insanity for political reasons 'in these ticklish times'. In 1689 he was created Duke of Bolton and began building a seat in neighbouring Wensleydale at Bolton Hall. He and his descendants were to own the mines through the crucial period of the next 150 years.

In 1700 a partnership headed by John Blackburne built a revolutionary Cupola smelt mill at Reels Head, close to Ince Wood above Marrick Priory. It used a reverberatory furnace to burn coal on a separate fire grate, reflecting heat onto the ore in a more efficient process and increasing the amounts that could be smelted in a single firing. In order to get a higher temperature, peat had to give way to coal from County Durham or from a pit at Burton Park in Wensleydale partially owned by Blackburne. It was not just coal that had to be carried a considerable distance, as the process was best run for long periods and ore was brought in from as far afield as a mine at Buckden in Upper Wharfedale.

It was another 90 years before the 5th Duke of Devonshire built a second Cupola mill in Yorkshire at Grassington. Unfortunately the pioneer at Marrick did not survive a protracted series of partnership disputes that broke out as early as 1704, the legal costs ultimately meaning that Blackburne lost his magnificent home at Friar's Head, near Winterburn in Malhamdale. In turn, the mill was in ruins by 1725 when it was demolished.

The mines on Hurst Moor prospered under Lord William Powlett, son of the Duke of Bolton, with a lease of 1717 including the proviso that at least 147 miners were to be employed. A resident steward was installed at newly built Hurst Hall, the centre of a mining settlement that gradually developed on the windswept heights some 1,200ft above sea level. It must often have been a grim existence, although a great annual occasion was Hurst Races in which only the horses of miners and carriers could participate.

Vigorous development continued through the latter part of the 18th and early 19th centuries and in 1817 the Powlett family sold Marrick Manor and its mines to Josias Morley of Beamsley Hall, near Skipton. His family remained owners through the rest of the mining era, although they also fought a continuous battle against debt. Josias died in 1827 when Francis, his son and heir, was only 14 and so trustees called in Captain John Harland of Reeth to manage the estate. He successfully cleared total liabilities of £26,000 [£2 million] through land sales and a more aggressive approach to the mining rights.

The mines were leased to Jaques & Co in 1828, the same year that they also took over Old Gang and thus now controlled an eight-mile length of all the richest mining on the north side of Swaledale. Disagreements meant that the lease lasted for only 14 years, although there was continued expansion during this period. By 1841 there was a peak population of 415 living in Hurst, the adjacent settlement of Washfold and the tiny nearby hamlet of Shaw. Ten years later there were 66 inhabited houses and those working at the mines included 12 male and 18 female ore dressers. Francis Morley had again accumulated debts to the extent that in 1848 he had fled the country and lived in France to avoid his creditors. His estate passed to his son, another Francis, who paid off some of these liabilities before escaping to Corfu in 1857.

On his return four years later a lease was drawn up with a new Hurst Mining Company headed by George Leeman, a York solicitor who had played a leading role in exposing the corrupt practices of George Hudson, the 'railway king'. On Hudson's dethronement, he was three times elected Lord Mayor of York and represented the city in Parliament. Leeman also had interests in ironstone mines in Cleveland and was well placed to guide the Hurst mines in the right direction. Output grew rapidly, peaking at 1,171 tons in 1867 and maintaining respectable figures through the difficult 1870s.

Production declined sharply at the end of this decade but there was to be one last burst of activity. Appointed resident agent was John Retallick, who hailed from Cornwall and was thus fully experienced in the use of steam power in mining operations. Hurst became the only Swaledale mines to make serious use of steam engines, beginning in 1883 with Cat Shaft with its round chimney far more characteristic of Cornwall than Yorkshire. It was followed four years later by Brown's New Engine Shaft, which created much interest when the boiler was brought up from Richmond. A team of 18 horses had to be augmented by even more on the steep climb out of Marske.

The miners were initially fortunate in encountering a fourteen-inch seam of coal above the lead veins, although supplies soon had to be obtained from Tan Hill or from pits in South Durham over 30 miles distant. Prolonged snowfall could cause delivery problems in the winter months. Yet the overall outlook seemed promising, as apart from Arkengarthdale the Hurst mines were now the only large producers left in Swaledale. Output rose to unusually high levels for the 1880s and reached 1,003 tons in 1887, but the continuing decline in lead prices coupled with under-funded development costs meant that it was but a brief moment of optimism. Trading ceased in 1890 and Francis Morley, now a Major-General, died two years later with a debt of £8,000 [£775,000] still outstanding.

Villages such as Gunnerside had already suffered with the cessation of mining but Hurst was in a different league. Owing its existence solely to the mines and developed alongside them, it quickly faded into virtual oblivion. A sorry sight remained when it was visited in the early 1930s by Ella Pontefact, collecting material for her book *Swaledale*. She painted

This page: *Early photograph of Washfold hamlet at Hurst, with a two-storey house in the foreground still retaining its steeply-pitched thatched roof. Hurst Board School is on top of the hill and just visible to its right is a row of bee boles, which no doubt provided miners with very welcome heather honey. (Swaledale Museum Archive)*
Opposite: *Hurst was long a remote and forgotten hamlet after the collapse of lead mining and was seldom visited. These rare views taken in September 1942 capture the atmosphere of those years. The thatched house shown on this page has lost its roof and the same fate has befallen a cottage close to the ford in the lower picture. (Clive Torrens collection)*

some evocative word pictures:

'Hurst is a broken village, left bewildered, its reason for being gone... There are ruins everywhere, and the houses which are left intact seem to weep with them... Thatched roofs, sagging and hanging dejectedly over the edges, add to the gloom of Hurst... The hillside has been tossed and tumbled like the moors behind the Old Gang, and two now useless chimneys rise from the wreckage like tombstones... Hurst should be seen if only to realize again what the dale has lost. Time will cover the scars as it has covered the earlier ones, and only mounds remain to tell of what was once the life and meaning of the place.'

A little more than mounds have managed to survive but the end seemed not far off in 1972 when the population once numbered in hundreds was down to a mere 18. The Methodist chapel, built to hold some 300 worshippers, was seeing services once a month in the summer and most of the building had become a hostel. The Green Dragon, the only survivor of three pubs, had a certain appeal to the dedicated by its claim to be England's loneliest inn. Yet by the mid-1980s it had become a private house, the greater part of Washfold was a sea of nettles and the remains of Shaw hamlet were a sheep dipping station.

Much property has since been restored, but it is still possible to sense that few mining communities have met such a sorry end in quite the same way as Hurst. In its total isolation it is in every sense on a road to nowhere, undisturbed by through traffic and with just the bleating of sheep and calls of moorland birds breaking the silence. For those who believe in seeking a ghostly past, there can be no better place to experience the final chapter in Swaledale lead mining and its miners.

5. GREENHOW

Hurst in Swaledale and Greenhow above Nidderdale are at opposite corners of the Dales and might appear to have nothing in common. Yet they both shared a feature and in many ways a handicap not to be found elsewhere. Rather than evolving from long-established farming communities, they were created in hostile locations specifically to mine lead. Even though Greenhow was slightly the higher at 1,300ft above sea level, there was in reality little to distinguish the two during times of torrential rain or terrible gale that seemed to be the norm rather than the exception. In the days of proper winters they would often be cut off for weeks on end by snowdrifts up to twenty feet high and cloud cover could seem perpetual.

Both looked dejected and forlorn when lead mining collapsed, but one facet was to save Greenhow from becoming a ghost settlement in quite the same way as Hurst. Instead of being on a road to nowhere, it was on either side of a key link for travellers going back to monastic times when monks from Fountains Abbey came this way to reach their granges and lands in Wharfedale and beyond. This route later became a turnpike and then an important road in the car age. Today it helps to bring visitors to a massive landscape sculpture at appropriately named Coldstones Cut. Here they can peer down into a spectacular working quarry and on a clear day enjoy vistas way beyond Greenhow, although some of them may wonder why Yorkshire's highest village came to be there at all.

Coldstones falls within the high moorland of Greenhow Hill, most of which became part of Bewerley Manor following the Norman Conquest. It extended from the watershed down to the west side of the River Nidd at Pateley Bridge, with the monks of both Fountains and Byland abbeys exercising mineral rights. They were aware of valuable reserves of lead on the Hill, which they used for their own purposes and also sold further afield as a source of considerable income. A typical instance occurred in 1365 when two wagons, each with 10 oxen, left Coldstones conveying lead for Windsor Castle. They travelled by 'high and rocky mountains and muddy roads' to Boroughbridge, from where the lead could be taken by river to Hull and thence on to London.

After the dissolution of the monasteries in 1539, Bewerley Manor along with its mineral rights had a succession of owners. Then in 1604 their

Although damaged, this photograph captures something of the bleakness of Greenhow after the collapse of lead mining with derelict houses and tumbledown walls. It also portrays the scattered nature of settlement, which had its origins in an early 17th century lawsuit that resulted in random smallholdings for farmer-miners. (Clive Torrens collection)

legitimacy was contested by Sir Stephen Proctor in a lengthy dispute, which went before the Star Chamber. Progress was not helped when he was imprisoned in the Tower of London for misdeeds in collecting fines, but eventually a Chancery judgement in 1613 found in his favour. The agreement sought to protect miners living in the area with the proviso that dwellings could be erected for them on what was then manorial waste. In addition, land would be improved so that they could keep draught oxen and horses for maintaining the mines.

Proctor could now develop mining as he wished. He could also build houses, forming the basis of what was to become Greenhow village just to the west of Coldstones. It may have seemed an improbable site, but lead ore was close to the surface on limestone pasture offering good grazing despite the altitude. Thus began a settlement with houses seemingly planted at random and spaced well apart in a series of smallholdings as is still clearly evident today. Miners had the unusual luxury of being able to work lead virtually on their front doorstep as well as having space for a few sheep and cattle that was not available in the relatively narrow confines of Nidderdale's valley floor. It must have been a welcome change from climbing almost a thousand feet in a little over three miles from Pateley Bridge to Greenhow to find employment.

Troubled times

The west side of the Greenhow watershed fell within the manor of Appletreewick, which similarly was worked by the monks of Bolton Priory. At the dissolution it was sold by Henry VIII for £14 10s [£7,500], only for it twice to be sold on during the same year, first for £666 [£348,000] and then after just two weeks for £1,000 [£523,000]. Land speculation is nothing new. Ten years later in it was bought for £2,000 [£810,000] by Sir John Yorke, who evicted 'evil-disposed persons' obtaining lead within its boundaries. In 1547 he had already purchased the former Byland Abbey estates of Stonebeck Up and Down, north of Pateley Bridge, for some £2,200 [£1 million].

It must have helped that Sir John was then in a position of power as nephew of the Duke of Somerset, guardian of the young King Edward VI. He was appointed a Sheriff of London in 1549, two years before he became Master of the Royal Mint, although fortunes soon changed in those turbulent times. His life looked like coming to an abrupt close in 1553 when he was thrown into the Tower of London for supporting Lady Jane Grey. Spared from execution and pardoned, his successors went on to retain ownership of Appletreewick Manor and its mineral rights for the next 450 years through to the present day.

Mining on Craven Moor adjoining the boundary with Bewerley manor was developed under leases from the Yorkes, although the lack of surface water

Sir John Yorke c1490 – 1568, who in 1549 bought Appletreewick Manor and thus the mineral rights on land immediately west of the Greenhow watershed. Four years later he found himself in the Tower of London for supporting Lady Jane Grey but was spared execution. (courtesy Charlie Yorke)

John Yorke 1733 – 1813 invested in Greenhow mining ventures, as well as acting as trustee for essential transport links such as the Grassington to Pateley Bridge turnpike and the Ripon Canal. His dislike of pomp was reflected in his portrait, when he chose to look like a gamekeeper (right) sitting on the ground next to his more ostentatious friend Colonel Coore. (courtesy Charlie Yorke)

meant it was impossible to provide a smelt mill. It was well that Sir John Yorke, grandson of the earlier Sir John, had in 1598 secured an agreement that ore could be carted through Greenhow village and down to Pateley Bridge to be smelted in Nidderdale. The Yorkes were a leading Catholic family in the dangerous days of Queen Elizabeth I and anathema to Sir Stephen Proctor, a staunch Protestant obsessed with stamping out recusancy. Any negotiations to take ore through Bewerley Manor would surely have proved hopeless once Proctor had claimed its ownership in 1604.

A relative newcomer in what was regarded as Yorke country, Proctor was a puritan among papists but was not to be deterred. He was eventually successful in implicating Yorke in the Gunpowder Plot leading to his incarceration in the Fleet prison for almost two years. By now the boundary at Greenhow separating Appletreewick and Bewerley must have been akin to a Middle East frontier where conflicting religions meet in hate and suspicion. Certainly the hostilities descended from the owners to the tenants, as instanced when those of Yorke threatened a wife in Bewerley with the taunt: 'Your husband shall have his nose slit, his ears cut off and preach at St Paul's Cross with a paper on his head!'

Such bitterness scarcely helped the development of lead mining, but both nationally and locally there were soon portents of a more stable future. By the late 17th century Britain was a country divided by political party rather than by creed. The Yorke family recovered after John's release and payment of substantial fines, and the cause of so much trouble ebbed away when Proctor sold Bewerley Manor. A final irony is that later generations of Yorkes were Protestants.

Dry Gill, next door to the Moorcock pub on the western edge of Greenhow, in an age when horses were essential. An early example of their key role was provided on 13th June 1776 when a horse and rider took an urgent letter from John Thornhill of Greenhow to George Bradley of Grassington regarding a meeting the following day. It may even have been more reliable than today's 1st Class Post! (David Dean collection)

Peak years

As elsewhere, greater economic activity in the 18th century meant that Greenhow benefited from the upsurge in mineral working. It was claimed that in 1735 the Yorke mines notched up sales of £8,000 [£1,100,000] and set a record never to be equalled. Adventurers came to Greenhow from other established mining areas, not just in the Dales at Grassington and Swaledale, but also from further afield. Among them was William Hutchinson from the Alston Moor mining field, who prospered sufficiently to be called a gentleman in 1782 instead of a miner as in 1770.

There was also Isaac Thornhill, a yeoman who came to Greenhow from Derbyshire and drove a level named after him. He was followed by the John Thornhill involved in a dispute at Coalgrovehead mine at Grassington. In June 1776 he wrote a letter to George Bradley, the Grassington Barmaster responsible for allocating ground to prospective miners. It must have been delivered from Greenhow by horse rider and very much captures the spirit of the times:

'Sir,

I cannot possibly come to Grassington yet am very desirous of half an hour's conversation with you concerning Colgrovehead Lead Mines. Would take it as a particular Favour if you would eat a Bitt of Mutton with me tomorrow being our pay day at Greenhough and take an opportunity from business after dinner to talk the affair over or I would willingly meet you as far from this place as I can walk say at Nursa House or if it can be convenient to you to call on me on Saturday or Sunday provided Friday is not convenient I will be very glad to see you.' [Nursa House is today Nussey House Farm on the main road to Grassington, 2½ miles from the centre of Greenhow village.]

A new era had certainly dawned when the Yorke family and Sir Thomas White, who had become the owner of Bewerley, drew up plans for joint working of their mines. Interlocking partnerships were formed among their lessees, although there was a limit as to how far harmony could proceed without grief. Linking the Craven Moor mines with an existing level at Cockhill, north of Greenhow village in Bewerley Manor, made eminent sense. In draining them it would permit working to a greater depth and allow ore to be taken by a more direct route to a smelt mill on the south side of Ashfoldside Gill, which was on the Byland Abbey estate bought by Sir John Yorke in 1547.

Yet the work was long delayed by disputes over wayleaves and boundaries, which were all too frequent and not always resolved in an orderly manner. When Samuel Swire was called in to settle a boundary quarrel, it was noted that he was 'detained at the public house at Greenhow Hill, where parties made him drunk and he gave his award under their influence without even having seen the spot'.

The necessity of mining at a deeper level increased capital costs and led to partnerships with a diverse range of shareholders to spread the risks in highly speculative investment. One example in 1783 involved four master linen weavers, two malsters, a tallow chandler, a saddler, a carrier and a lead miner. The chief partner William Wood held a one-eighth share, as did a later John Yorke as lessor. (Nearly all the Yorke first sons were christened John.)

Wood was the main investor when in 1781 a rich strike of ore on Craven Moor reputedly yielded profits in excess of £20,000 [£2¼ million] in three years. Then water overwhelmed the workings so suddenly that the miners had to escape with great haste and leave all tools and ore behind. Craven Moor presented formidable difficulties, as rain disappeared into the limestone and waterwheels were thus impracticable. It was a situation that led to a brief association with some of the most famous names in the history of steam power.

Wood decided to pump water out of the mine on the Craven Cross vein with a beam engine and turned for advice to the noted Yorkshire engineer, John Smeaton. Attempts to persuade James Watt to visit the site were unsuccessful but an order was nevertheless placed with the recently established firm of Boulton & Watt, destined to play a major role in the industrial revolution. Delivery of the first steam engine to be used at the Greenhow mines took place in November 1785. Peat was dug to fire it, although it seems likely it would have to be mixed with coal brought from Aket Colliery at Grimwith. Its quality did not impress Smeaton, who described it as 'small and drossy, like the Welsh coals carried to Cornwall, but without their bituminous quality'.

An alternative source was good-quality coal from collieries in the Leeds area, conveyed via the Leeds & Liverpool Canal after it had reached Skipton in 1777. It could be bought for about 8s 6d a ton [£49], but cost at least twice this sum by the time it reached Greenhow. This was despite transport charges being reduced through coal representing 'back carriage' for wagons taking corn from Ripon to Skipton. Lead from Greenhow seldom went this way, instead going over to the Ripon Canal created under a 1759 Act of Parliament and showing just how far the influence of key local families then extended. The trustees included Thomas and John Yorke and John Smeaton was the engineer.

This John Yorke was also trustee of the turnpike linking Grassington with Pateley Bridge, authorised in 1759 when the existing road was in 'ruinous condition' and was also 'very narrow and inconvenient, especially for wheeled traffic'. The specification that 'all the ascents shall be made easy and regular' was clearly impossible, but on just the short stretch between Greenhow and Pateley the initial outlay on surfacing was an expensive £160 [£22,000] per mile. Annual income between 1801 and 1810 was only some £8 [£580] per mile, one problem being that lead ore carried to smelt mills was exempt from tolls. A clause to this effect had been stipulated by the trustees, so perhaps John Yorke took a rounded view and accepted the substantial losses thus incurred.

The turnpike nevertheless helped growth of the scattered settlement at its Greenhow summit and encouraged men with wider mining experience to move into the area. In 1820 a Ripon parish record described Greenhow as 'a large straggling village, upon an eminence, abounding with lead mines and in which there are rarely less than five hundred inhabitants employed'. It noted that mines with the colourful names of Sunside, Prosperous, Providence, Cockhill and Merryfield were annually producing about 2,000 tons of lead.

Chapel and Church

Cynics might argue that those living high on Greenhow were closer to heaven and thus needed less spiritual guidance. Others would aver their surroundings were so harsh that every comfort was required. Whatever the case, as early as 1689 a Presbyterian meeting house had been licensed in the home of Philip Harrap, who had married the daughter of Captain Richard Freeman – a former officer in Cromwell's army. It survived until about 1770.

As elsewhere, Methodism appealed to the independent spirit of the miners and became established amid much hostility. The first meetings were in houses or barns with preachers often facing danger and hardship as they did their missionary work. Thomas Lee was more than once attacked by an organised mob in Pateley Bridge on his way up to Greenhow. In 1752 he was pulled off his horse, dragged into the main sewer and then thrown into the river. His wife received several blows on the head and was left bleeding at the mouth. The activities of Francis Darnbrook, an early Methodist adherent living on Greenhow, led to him being dismissed from his work and turned off some land he rented.

Darnbrook became a trustee of a new Wesleyan chapel opened in Pateley Bridge in 1760, as did William Wood of the Craven Moor mining enterprises. The seating arrangements specifically segregated the sexes but at least there was provision for women to attend. One can only ponder on the arrangements when the powerful evangelist, Mary Barritt, had the

Greenhow looking west. On the right is the Methodist Chapel of 1812, which pre-dated St Mary's Church of 1858 just visible on the skyline. (Greenhow Local History Club)

Once there were three pubs on Greenhow and now there are none. The Miners' Arms, the main one of the three, was noted for vigorous argument on anything from sheep prices to the richest lead ever found! (Ben McKenzie collection)

courage to preach on Greenhow in May 1793 at the age of just twenty-one. She noted in her journal that 'some lasting good was done', although only ten years later the Wesleyan movement forbade women to preach other than to their own sex – and then only in exceptional circumstances.

Greenhow got its own chapel in 1812 at a cost of £420 [£25,000]. It had 41 members – the second highest number on the Pateley Bridge circuit – and this grew over the ensuing years. The 1851 religious census showed attendances of 128 at its afternoon service and in addition there were 52 Sunday scholars. Music was provided by a 17-strong brass brand, which was far from happy when an organ was installed.

Not until 1858 did the village get St Mary's Church, rather dismissively described by the Nidderdale historian William Grainge as 'a small unpretending fabric'. An incoming vicar was once greeted with a barbed Yorkshire welcome: 'It's as near heaven as ever you'll get!' A separate graveyard was entered by a lychgate with an inscription from the Psalms: 'I will lift up mine eyes unto the hills from whence cometh my help.' Its aptness was sometimes queried on the grounds that those on Greenhow looked down rather than up. A recreation room, opened in 1863, provided newspapers to keep parishioners in touch with the outside world and offered games such as chess and draughts. By this date there were also

The two teachers and 37 pupils of Greenhow School about 1895 when numbers had slumped from a peak of around the 200 mark. The collapse of an attempted mining revival in the 1930s led to its closure in 1941. (David Dean collection)

three public houses – the Miner's Arms, Queen's Head and the Moorcock – and the shops included an all-important grocer. Perhaps the biggest surprise of all in such a location was a bowling green.

All must have seemed well in a flourishing community with some 80 houses nearly all occupied by miners, but not for the first time the village was becoming immersed in a bitter religious divide. It centred round events of about 1812 when a later John Yorke contributed towards 'building a school for the poor and ignorant children on Greenhow Hill'. Irrespective of their religious denomination, volunteers carted stones and raised about £300 in subscriptions. It was a non-sectarian school run by a predominantly Methodist community, a state of affairs that caused trouble in many mining villages when the Church of England attempted to re-assert its authority in the second half of the 19th century.

In 1878 the *Nidderdale Herald* claimed that the John Yorke of the day had seized control of the school. Its intellectual standing had accordingly been lost, as any child who did not attend a C of E Sunday school was refused admission. It says much for Victorian principles and verbosity that a formal proposal was made to attach the school to the worthily titled National Society for the Education of the Poor in the Principles of the Established Church. There would be a proviso that nonconformist children could be withdrawn from religious instruction. Not surprisingly there was intense local opposition and the idea was abandoned.

Final fling

Issues centred on the school eventually settled down, although the introduction of compulsory education in 1880 meant that at times it could be extremely cramped. Pupil numbers rose to close on 200 but this peak was not to last. The pattern seen elsewhere was followed and an abrupt decline meant that by 1895 the Greenhow mining field was at a standstill. The end seemed nigh but unique circumstances were to prolong the quest for lead longer than in most parts of the Dales. It was the age when Bradford was wool capital of the world and needed ever increasing amounts of water for its mills. In the closing years of the 19th century it embarked on an ambitious scheme to build Angram and Scar House reservoirs at the head of Nidderdale and supply the city's needs through a pipeline running under Greenhow at a depth of 400 feet. Completed in 1899, this 3.8 mile tunnel not only encountered veins of good-quality ore but also provided drainage that would enable the mines to be worked to a much greater depth.

Nothing practical was done until the rising price of lead in World War One caused mines to be reopened. These were difficult days but miners again responded to the challenge. In the coal strike of 1919 steam engines at two shafts on Craven Moor were kept running solely on peat, which fortunately was exceptionally dry due to a long summer drought. Various ventures continued intermittently with about 1,000 tons of ore being raised in 1928, although Greenhow no longer had a smelting mill in working order and it had instead to be sent to Newcastle.

In 1933 a new dressing plant was built at Cockhill but revival was decidedly hit-and-miss, as reflected in numbers at the village school. Peak years had given way to a sharp decline by the early 1920s when the late revival of mining saw an upturn until the mid-1930s. It was not to last, the increasingly troubled times in Europe contributing to a decline in lead prices. The school closed in 1941, three years after operations ceased at Cockhill, and was converted into cottages.

Workings after World War Two increasingly involved fluorspar rather than just lead. Yet the underground search continued until the late 1960s, although the numbers so employed were now tiny. At least it had all lasted long enough to avoid Greenhow village being totally abandoned. Old miners continued to live in some cottages, while derelict properties saw gradual restoration as part of a new fashion for weekend homes. Others became permanent residences for hardy and determined people able to cope with savage gales, biting cold and no sun for days or sometimes weeks on end.

The written word

Greenhow held a fascination with writers well before the mines went into terminal decline. Two of the most noted were coincidentally born in India within nine years of one another. By far the most famous was immensely popular in the late 19th and early 20th centuries for his short stories and passionate chronicling of the British Empire. Rudyard Kipling, born in Bombay in 1865, was the first English-language writer to be awarded the Nobel Prize for Literature. It surprises many that someone so elevated in the literary world should choose to weave words round Greenhow, but in fact he was familiar with the area as his grandfather was superintendent of Pateley Bridge Methodist circuit. His skills were already evident when at the age of 23 he penned 'Greenhow Hill', included in his *Soldiers Three* collection of short stories. It set the scene admirably:

> *'Moors and moors and moors, with never a tree for shelter, and grey houses with flagstone roofs, and pewits crying, and a windhover going too and fro. And cold! You can tell Greenhow folk by the red apple colour of their cheeks and nose tips, and their blue eyes, driven into pinpoints by the wind. Miners mostly, burrowing for lead in the hillsides, following the trail of the ore vein same as a field rat. It was the roughest mining I had ever seen. You'd come on a bit of creaking wood windlass, like a well-head, and you was let down in the bight of a rope, fending yourself off the side with one hand, carrying a candle stuck in a lump of clay with the other... And then you came to a level, where you crept on your hands and knees through a mile of winding drift, and you came into a cave place as big as Leeds Town Hall, with an engine pumping water from workings that went deeper still.'*

The extreme step has been taken of adjusting the original dialect in this quotation to suit today's reader. It is a liberty that would have appalled the redoubtable Harald John Lexow Bruff, born in Akra in 1874, who became secretary and treasurer of the Yorkshire Dialect Society. At the age of 29 he married a Norwegian and later bought her a house on Greenhow. She initially refused to live in what she dismissed as 'that godforsaken place' but eventually relented. Bruff came to play a major role in the mining revival during World War One and set about recording detailed memories recounted by miners, their parents and their grandparents. Ultimately he

Harald Bruff 1874 – 1946, a leading exponent of Yorkshire dialect also spearheaded the revival of mining on Greenhow during World War One. His notebooks and photographs of miners during this critical period form a fascinating record, which is now in the Special Collections Department at Leeds University Library. (Ernest Busfield collection)

was a pioneer of what he termed 'gramophonic recording of dialects', but this belonged to the future when in 1920 he set down the miners' tales in two books of character sketches largely written in dialect.

Today they are not an easy read and his view of those who failed to settle on Greenhow is scarcely acceptable: 'The selfish ones, the timid and the craven ones, the lazy and the slothful ones the Hill had no use for, and drove them down and back to where they came from, the stew-kettles of humanity, the towns, that distil vice and passions.'

Yet for those who persevere there is much in Bruff's books that vividly captures the customs, traditions and beliefs of their time. The main pub was then the Miners' Arms, where those present often sat for hours on end without uttering a word. They were not there solely for the sake of the beer but it was their 'exchange' for news, prices of beasts, sheep and fodder, and in olden days the prospects of striking it rich in the mines. Sadness about a disappearing way of life was well conveyed in *T'ill an' T'oade Uns upuv Grenho*:

> *'Yes! They were men like towers, but they are nearly all gone now. It was inevitable that these men should disappear when the mines, its sole industry and means of existence for nearly all of them stopped. There were a few who had a little patch of land and owned a few beasts, and these managed to remain fighting a losing fight for their existence.'*

Harald Bruff felt the need for somewhere for Greenhow locals to get together and in 1939 bought a wooden building from Scar House reservoir site to use as a village institute. He had it re-erected and added a plaque paying tribute to Thomas Blackah, the 'Miners' Poet'. Such an action was understandable as Blackah was a Greenhow miner born in 1827 who 40 years later had printed a book *Songs and Poems in the Nidderdale Dialect*. The poems were written about the people he knew and one tells of those who moved away when the mines started to close. Blackah was himself a restless traveller reputedly living in 17 different houses in 17 years. In the best tradition of miners, he spent his spare time knitting woollen socks and was noted as a 'sweet singer'.

Much dialect writing is now unfashionable. It may also seem flowery, but in this respect there is no equal to the prose of Halliwell Sutcliffe, high priest of Dales romanticism, whose 1929 book *The Striding Dales* had much to say about Greenhow – 'a strange, desolate country, whose loneliness seems only deepened by the unsheltered road that winds through it, a narrow ribbon of grey'.

Sutcliffe averred that 'wherever one wanders across these highlands, the mine-pits lie in wait; and the story of each deserted shaft, if its mouldering props and beams could speak, would be an epic of hard strife, of courage that thought little of itself – and of ghostly happenings that were real as daily toil'. And so it continues for page after page, giving full vent to goblins, mysterious tappings underground and 'lanterns playing peep-a-boo with the dark across the silent pastures'.

Quite what Greenhow miners made of it all is perhaps best left to the imagination, especially as hope for the future was fast ebbing. It was a sorry tale in April 1937 when a *Yorkshire Evening Post* journalist 'discovered' Jim Simpson, aged 70, eking out his last days at a lonely farm near Cockhill. His ancestors had all been tenants of royalty owner Sir Thomas White in 1801 and fifty years later there were 55 Simpsons living on Greenhow, but Jim was the only member of the family listed as a lead miner in the 1901 census. His mind was still clear and he lamented how in two years he had lost four cows and 20 sheep due to lead poisoning. He preferred to talk about a past life that was even harder:

'I never went to school. There wasn't time nor money for it. What I know I learnt at my mother's knee, and I went into my first job, at the Cockhill smelting mill, when I was 10. It was terrible hard work and dangerous too. We used to have to be stripped to the waist. Clothes would get scorched and spattered with flying splashes of molten lead if you wore them, and sweat would roll off you in streams.'

Jim later became the last smelter to work at Heathfield mill, the final Dales smelt mill to close in 1909:

> *'It was a hard life. We worked six days a week and we were on piecework. We had to get out eight pigs of lead a day. If the ore was good and they had got all the muck out of it then it would take five hours. If it was dirty, it might take seven or eight hours. Squire Yorke exacted a royalty in kind. He took one pig of lead weighing about eight stone in every 20 produced. They used to clean the flue out each year-end and I have seen as much as 20 tons of lead come out of it. That all belonged to Mr Yorke as well.'*

Jim cherished the hope that lead mining on Greenhow would resume in earnest but the closure of operations at Cockhill a year later effectively spelt the end. It was left to the noted social historian Marie Hartley to write a suitable epitaph in 1940:

> *'A climb up Greenhow Hill brings abundant signs in the heaps and hollows of old workings on the moors, the levels running into the mines, the smelting chimneys and the ruins of smelt mills. Time may remove these signs, dispel the spirits of the old miners haunting the moors, kill the legends of strange knockings by which long dead miners warned their descendants of coming danger, but the village of Greenhow will remain as a memorial to the industry to which it owes its existence.'*

6. GRASSINGTON

L ittle more than five miles separate the lead mines of Grassington from those of Greenhow, but despite their closeness there was one fundamental difference. Rather than lessees, its key mines were worked and extensively developed by the owner, who was no ordinary investor. The mineral rights came into possession of the richest dukedom in England. In the halcyon years of expansive output in the mid-19th century, miners in Grassington may not have doffed their caps but must have felt they owed much to what seemed to be the limitless resources of the 6th Duke of Devonshire.

The saga began over 200 years earlier. Lead ore was discovered on the moor north of the village and efforts to extract it were made by George Clifford, 3rd Earl of Cumberland. He had inherited some 90,000 acres of land rewarded to his predecessors by grateful sovereigns and his estate embraced Skipton Castle and virtually the whole of Craven. It thus included the Manor of Grassington – and hence its mineral rights.

A trusted member of the court of Queen Elizabeth I, the Earl equipped no less than eleven expeditions sailing to various far-flung parts of the world. Noted for his buccaneering spirit, he also indulged in unsuccessful privateering ventures and had a gambling streak typical of the times. His famous daughter Lady Anne Clifford was critical of his favourite activities such as 'horse racing, tilting, shooting, bowling matches and all such expensive sports'. In 1604 his mounting debts forced most of the Grassington land to be sold to sitting tenants but he retained the mineral rights. As part of an effort to raise money, skilled miners were brought into the village and in the following year a smelt mill was built close to the river.

Mining was not greatly developed by his successor Francis Clifford, the 4th Earl, who in 1618 ceased direct involvement in searching for lead ore and put prospecting out to lessees. Working was governed by the Barmoot, a court set up to handle administration and any disputes that arose. In turn the Earl appointed a Barmaster, who was responsible for allocating ground to groups of prospective miners and determining the amount of royalty they had to pay.

There were soon more serious matters in these troubled times. The Cliffords were staunch Royalists and Skipton Castle was besieged by Parliamentarian forces for three years until its garrison surrendered in December 1645. The 5th and last Earl died in the midst of it all in 1643 and the Grassington mineral rights were among the part of his estate that passed to his daughter Elizabeth. She had already improved her lot by marrying Richard Boyle, the 2nd Earl of Corke and Earl of

Burlington, whose vast Irish estates had been bought at a knockdown price from Sir Walter Raleigh while he was in prison.

The 3rd Earl of Burlington had no male heir and his daughter Charlotte was thus among the most eligible of young women when at the age of 16 she agreed in 1748 to marry William Cavendish, 28 year old son of the 3rd Duke of Devonshire. Already one of the great Whig families of Georgian England with a 'country palace' at Chatsworth in Derbyshire, the Cavendishes had a reputation for marrying into the aristocracy with the intention of obtaining land. They now undoubtedly gained the most substantial of all matrimonial additions to their property. When the 3rd Earl died in 1753 he left a castle and several thousand acres in southern Ireland, rich agricultural land in the East Riding of Yorkshire, a palatial house in London's Piccadilly and a large villa on the Thames at Chiswick. Lower down the scale were what had been the Clifford lands around Skipton and Bolton Abbey. These included the Grassington mineral rights, which had thus twice descended through an heiress. They were now destined to remain with successive Dukes of Devonshire until the present day, meaning that in over four centuries they have been owned by only three families.

The collective riches were not to be long enjoyed by Lady Charlotte. She conceived four children in the space of six years and was again pregnant when she died of smallpox at the age of 22 in 1754. Her husband became the 4th Duke of Devonshire the following year on the death of his father and was briefly 'the most reluctant and uncomfortable Prime Minister in English history'. He died young in 1763 when their son was still a minor. The dukedom was thus effectively mothballed for the next seven years until at the age of 21 the 5th Duke found himself one of the richest and most extensive landowners in Britain.

Yet he seemed to be crushed beneath the sheer weight of his inheritance. Noted as lethargic and indecisive, the Duke's ultimate misfortune was that nothing really mattered and his favourite occupation was spending the night whiling away boredom by drinking and gambling in London clubs. He parted with huge sums as did his infamous first wife – the celebrated beauty and society hostess Lady Georgiana Spencer, who in 15 years managed to run up gaming debts of at least £60,000 [£6½ million].

It was fortunate that unexpected mineral wealth came the Duke's way – not from distant Grassington but closer to Chatsworth at Ecton in Staffordshire's Manifold Valley. Vast deposits of high-grade copper ore were found in what at over 1,200ft was claimed to be the world's then deepest mine. They contributed to Britain's position as the number one supplier of copper and in just eight years in the 1780s produced profits of £186,000 [£21 million]. Apart from no doubt helping at the gaming tables, they also created a permanent legacy in financing the building of Buxton's magnificent Crescent.

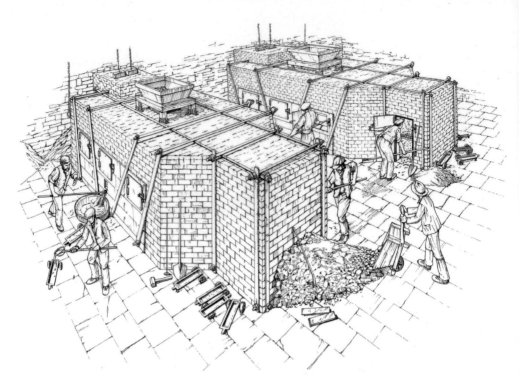

The impressive Cupola smelt mill built by the 5th Duke of Devonshire on the edge of Grassington Out Moor in 1792. It had two furnaces which burnt coal and could run continuously.

Slow change

Ecton copper mine suddenly failed in 1790. It was a disaster that may well have finally turned the attention of the Duke and his advisors to Grassington, where mining had been left to follow its old ways and no attempt made to maximise revenue. Barmasters continued to handle working by small partnerships, allotting ground in 'meers' 30 yards long and 30 yards wide marked initially by stakes and later by inscribed meer stones. Increasing numbers of shallow shafts were sunk on the Old Pasture around Yarnbury, 1½ miles north-east of Grassington village, and then spread further east to either side of New Pasture Beck and the Out Moor stretching over towards the watershed with Nidderdale. Miners were poorly paid on a piecework basis with the partnerships often financed by local worthies. Typical of them was Henry Wickham, Justice of the Peace and Overseer of the Poor. The same roles were fulfilled by P.W. Overend, whose family was later part of Overend, Gurney & Co which succumbed in one of the most disastrous banking crashes of the 19th century.

Two years after the failure at Ecton, a new wave of expansion seemed to be dawning. A reverberatory smelt mill, similar to the pioneer example near Hurst in Swaledale, was built in 1792 on the edge of the Out Moor immediately east

Coal for the new smelt mill reached Skipton via the eastern section of the Leeds & Liverpool Canal completed in 1777. Lead was taken out in the reverse direction and often transshipped at Leeds, where as seen here there was generally a busy scene at the intersection with the Aire Navigation.

of Hebden Gill. In reality it was primarily a response to constant complaints and threats from Grassington freeholders, who rightly claimed that peat being used in existing ore-hearth mills belonged to them through ancient rights of turbary. An additional difficulty was that bad management of Grass Wood had led to a shortage of kindling.

High-quality coal needed for the new mill's two furnaces could now more readily be obtained following completion in 1777 of the eastern end of the Leeds & Liverpool Canal, which linked Skipton with collieries in the industrial West Riding. It also eased the dispatch of lead to distant markets as it connected with the Aire Navigation and hence Hull.

Output from Grassington ought to have markedly improved but instead it went into gradual decline. Shallow shafts had given way to extensive workings at Coalgrovebeck on the Out Moor after 1756, when William Brown, a colliery viewer from the north-east, installed pumps that enabled rich ore to be found at a 300ft depth. Yet within 20 years these workings were flooded and the overall outlook was far from promising. After almost two centuries, prospecting had left very few new and accessible veins to be discovered and the existing partnerships had neither the resources nor the will to explore further. The water table had been reached and the only way forward was massive investment in pumping or drainage.

In his usual diffident way, the Duke showed considerable hesitation before he agreed in 1796 to build a deep level, well over a mile in length, that would drain both the Yarnbury and Out Moor mines and more than double the depth to which they could be worked. Even this proved to be flawed in concept. Cornelius Flint, the Mineral Agent responsible for all his mining affairs, came up with a plan that with hindsight verged on the edge of lunacy.

Flint was influenced by fashionable ideas for underground canals pioneered by the Duke of Bridgewater at Worsley, near Manchester, and John Smeaton at Alston in Cumberland. He wanted the new level to be 9ft high and 5ft wide so that it could be more than merely a drain and would enable ore to be fetched out in small barges or tubs. Thomas Bowdin was brought in from Ecton to act as local agent for the project working alongside George Bradley, the Barmaster. Starting from a point in Hebden Gill, one of the greatest and yet largely unseen projects of its time encountered hard rock but despite its excessive dimensions still progressed at what was considered a respectable five feet per week.

Anxious times

In the meantime the lead mines remained virtually dormant and many miners in Grassington village must have had time on their hands. The 1803 muster roll for militia service, drawn up in readiness for Napoleonic invasion, shows that they comprised more than half the working population and far outnumbered other occupations. There were 75 miners compared with only 12 farmers, while the four carters, three carpenters and three smelters had direct links with the lead industry. So too did six blacksmiths, who would be almost entirely employed in making tools and shoeing horses for the mines. All those involved in the quest for lead needed feeding and clothing, and hence there was a shopkeeper, a butcher, two tailors, a clogger and a shoemaker. This was a village that lived by the lead mines and it must have been deeply worried.

The Established Church offered little comfort. The Reverend Doctor Thomas Dunham Whitaker was just completing his monumental work *The History and Antiquities of the Deanery of Craven* and in the Grassington section did at least acknowledge the existence of lead mining:

> *'The first discoveries of this valuable metal consisted in great perpendicular trunks of ore called pipes, which sometimes appeared on the surface, and conducted the fortunate discoverer to sudden wealth without skill, and almost without effort. When these were exhausted, the spirit of adventure, which they had excited, continued to the ruin of many families. For henceforward the veins of ore, irregular and capricious in their ramifications, gradually diminished, while the cost of pursuing them increased.'*

Yet as a firm believer in a divine class structure his concerns were limited to ruination of the local gentry rather than what he termed 'the mere trash of a churchyard'. In extreme views that were to be perpetuated in his later History of Richmondshire, the reverend doctor concluded: 'I do not know a greater calamity which can befall a village than the discovery of a lead mine in the neighbourhood.'

Grassington fell within the ecclesiastical parish of Linton and its inhabitants may not have fully recovered from the 40-year reign of its rector, the Rev Benjamin Smith. A nephew of Sir Isaac Newton and a Fellow of Pembroke Hall, Cambridge, he regarded the living of a remote Dales parish as totally beneath his dignity and spent long hours in bed listening to Latin and Greek read by his manservant. Fellow clerics may have been guilty of a sneer when they commented that he was one of the best dancers in England and they could not forgive the way he despised his parishioners and regarded them as 'baptised brutes'.

It is scarcely surprising that John Wesley had received rapt attention from 'a great crowd' of miners and other villagers when in 1780 he stopped to preach on his way from Skipton to Pateley Bridge. He came again two years later and a Methodist chapel was duly opened in 1809. The Independents were stirred into action and replaced previous meetings in private houses with their own chapel, which held its first service on Christmas Day 1811. It later became the Congregational Chapel.

Five months earlier there may well have been mixed feelings in the village following the death of the 5th Duke of Devonshire. His successor at the age of 21, the 6th 'Bachelor Duke', had an income of about £70,000 (£4½ million) per year but thanks to fecklessness by both his father and mother he also inherited £500,000 (£20 million)

The Congregational Chapel (right), opened in 1811, and Chapel House. (David Dean collection)

95

of debt. Yet he seemed not to be prone to their reckless extravagances and there was hope that change for the better might be on the horizon. Driving of the deep level was still dragging its weary way and at first it seemed little could be done to restore mining fortunes until it was further advanced. Output continued to fall and in 1816 reached its lowest level for almost a century. The Duke had had enough and dismissed William Sheffield who had succeeded Cornelius Flint as Mineral Agent.

Radical reform

The Duke now turned to John Taylor, a mining engineer and prodigy in his field, who in 1798 at the age of only nineteen had transformed operations when he was appointed manager of Wheal Friendship, one of Devon's largest copper mines. Destined to create an impressive business empire and revolutionise mining on an international scale, he was invited to visit Grassington in January 1818. Before the end of the month the Duke took a decisive step he can never have regretted and Taylor became his new Mineral Agent.

In modern jargon, Taylor was headhunted and like a present-day newly appointed chief executive he wasted no time in making radical changes. Immediately reviewing the progress on Duke's Level with Thomas Bowdin, he found that it had reached the Yarnbury veins after being driven for a little over 4,100ft at a cost of £19,275 [£1¼ million]. He concluded that not only was this too expensive but the project was ill-conceived, as the ore brought out by boat would then have to be carted up the valley to be dressed close to the existing smelt mill. This would far exceed the cost of drawing it to the surface through shafts. Within a week of taking up his appointment, Taylor gave instructions that work on the Level would continue at normal dimensions of 6ft 6in high by 4ft 6in wide.

In order to spread risk, Taylor continued the traditional practice of leasing many mines on the Out Moor to partnerships or companies, thus incurring no development costs and at the same time receiving duty payments. More fundamentally, he took an opposite approach with the mines at Yarnbury and Coalgrovebeck. The Duke, via his Agent, became an 'Adventurer', directly investing in them to increase efficiency and profitability.

Transforming the fortunes of a mining field that had been neglected for some 40 years involved immense effort, determination and expense. Improved pumping and winding arrangements were provided at deeper shafts with waterwheels fed by over six miles of watercourses from newly constructed dams at Blea Beck on the east side of the Out Moor. These shafts were linked by roads and railways to more centralised dressing floors where grinding mills were built to crush the ore. The more easily graded Duke's New Road was constructed from Yarnbury to the Out Moor, making it easier for carriers to take out the smelted lead. Horse-drawn carts would return with coal, which from 1819 largely came from Lancashire via

The massive waterwheel on Grassington Out Moor which pumped several nearby shafts. It was installed by John Taylor, who transformed the 6th Duke's mining operations.

a staith at Ray Bridge, near Gargrave, following completion of the western end of the Leeds & Liverpool Canal. As the mines expanded, the New Road also carried growing quantities of timber brought to a sawmill built to provide props and planks for supporting the workings. Practically all of this expansion was financed from income – mainly from the Yarnbury mines.

Taylor was fully aware that this investment would be wasted without a more organised and disciplined workforce functioning under his overall supervision. He sought men he knew to be talented, beginning in 1820 with John Barratt who had been a manager of mines at Tavistock in Devon and was especially skilled in ore dressing and use of water power. He became Taylor's northern consultant to oversee developments at Grassington and was provided with a stylish Georgian house purpose-built for him at Yarnbury. It also served as the mine offices in the new era of more dynamic management. Barratt cemented his links with the area by marrying the daughter of Joseph Mason, who had succeeded George Bradley as Barmaster.

A few miners' houses were provided at Yarnbury and on the Out Moor but the majority of men and boys continued to live in Grassington. Among them in 1820 was 11-year-old John Aldersley, whose father was a time-keeper at one of the dressing floors. The harsh working conditions made a vivid impression on him and much later in life he set down his memories in a journal:

> *'The men were always expected to get their work tools fixed and everything made
> ready to begin working their new places on a Monday morning, A sharp lookout was*

kept to see that every man was in his place. No man was allowed to lose a day without giving a reason for so doing. If he could not give a reason for his absence, he was fined and a paper was put on the door of the blacksmith shop on which was written a notice of the fine.'

John Aldersley noted that the amount involved in this humiliation was about the same as payment of 2s 6d [£9] for a day's labour. He was also fascinated by work at the smelt mill, where a new arrangement had provided for groups of miners to place their dressed ore in separate piles in a large walled compound:

'A day was appointed to weigh all the piles of ore. It took five or six men to weigh a pile of mineral. Two hundred pounds weight was weighed at each draft. Two men filled the ore into a handbarrow and two men carried it onto the scales and one man stood at the scales with shovel in hand. There was also a man with a book and pencil to mark down each barrow.'

Today it sounds like a case of serious over-manning but it was then seen as a first stage in introducing new methods at the smelt mill. As a next step, Taylor decided to improve quality control by bringing in a professional assayer able to analyse minerals and assess their respective values. It was again someone he knew. Edward Henry was the manager's son at a smelting works near Holywell in Flintshire, owned by Lord Grosvenor for whom Taylor had also served as Mineral Agent.

It took time for all the radical reforms and major investment to achieve results but by 1825 the mines were prospering and three-shift working was introduced. Each shift was a mandatory eight hours, although Barratt noted that the men had been 'very obstinate' in opposing such a system. It nevertheless helped the annual output of lead from Grassington to rise from a desultory 161 tons to more than 1000 tons in the ten years following Taylor's appointment. There was also a steady increase in the population of the village from 763 in 1801 to 1067 in 1831, although this expansion was then pegged by the slump in lead prices.

A time of reckoning came in 1830. The Yarnbury mines had over the last eight years incurred high development costs but had nevertheless achieved a modest overall profit of £652 [£52,000]. This was roughly in line with expectations and reflected the wisdom of Taylor's decision to reserve these workings for the Duke. Sadly, the position at Coalgrovebeck on the Out Moor was directly the opposite with a loss of £9,800 [£780,000] in the same period, as it had become increasingly clear that the richest deposits of ore had already been exhausted.

A dismal situation was compounded by a severe winter, reflected in letters written to Taylor by John Barratt between late December 1829 and February 1830. He noted that 'a great fall of snow' had stopped dressing and that he had

The few miners' cottages on the Out Moor included these close to Coalgrovebeck. (drawing by John Dean, courtesy David Dean)

'frequently observed a thermometer at 22 degrees [Fahrenheit] below the freezing point'. He concluded: 'A great many poor people employed on the surface will I am afraid from the length of time they have been hindered from their work be very much distressed.'

Several mining families felt the immediate future looked so bleak that they emigrated to America. Barratt was moved to propose a reduction in his salary and the Duke's financial advisors must have been worried men, especially as more losses were yet to come. The massive profits that lay ahead can scarcely have been anticipated. Completion of Duke's Level in 1830 at least facilitated drainage and deeper workings on the Out Moor, but the real stimulus was a gradual upturn in lead prices.

Full recovery took a decade, although a change that was to pay future dividends occurred in late 1833 or early the following year. Barratt had negotiated a lease of Coniston copper mine in the Lake District and moved there to become its manager. He was replaced by Cornish-born Stephen Eddy, whom Taylor moved from Lord Grosvenor's mines in Flintshire. A pioneer in the use of wire rope in British metal mines, he soon became the driving force at Grassington and especially development on the Out Moor. He also saw through major changes at the smelt mill, beginning in 1849 with the first stages of a complex system of flues and condensers linked to a tall chimney that today is the most striking remnant of the mining era.

Miners walk towards a condenser, which was packed with brushwood intended to trap poisonous fumes from the smelt mill. In the distance is the chimney, built by Stephen Eddy in 1849 as part of an overall scheme of improvements.

High noon

Mining output peaked in the first half of the 1850s, as did the population of Grassington. The 1851 census, more detailed than any of its predecessors, not only records 1138 inhabitants but also brings into sharper perspective the miners and their way of life. It helps to dispel a few legends, showing that this was not a population constantly on the move. The overwhelming majority of miners had been born in Grassington or its neighbouring villages, with just a few coming from other centres rich in lead ore such as Alston. It also shows that the era when women were working at the dressing floors had gone, which was certainly not the case in Swaledale, but boys as young as nine were still so employed.

Smelters continued to class themselves as a wholly separate occupation, as instanced by Thomas Worsley living up at Yarnbury. Here too – and perhaps still reflecting John Taylor's West Country connections – were mineral agents Sampson Mitchell, born in Devon, and Richard Williams from Calstock in Cornwall. The latter lived in a more comfortable style than most of his contemporaries and had both a housekeeper and a house servant to help look after his three young children.

Otherwise, almost all connected with lead mining were still living in Grassington village, even though the furthest workings now involved a daily journey of three miles each way on foot or horseback. They included 'miners agent' Joseph

Mason, whose father of the same name had earlier been Barmaster, and three smelters – James Blackey, George Lee and George Lodge, who was the only person in the census to record his sons as lead ore dressers. All the rest simply used the term lead miner, although a fortunate few among the total of 122 were smallholders farming a few acres.

The number of occupants in a house was frequently sizeable, as instanced in the home of miner William Simpson. He was married to Nancy, who would have intrigued latter-day feminists by listing her occupation as 'Wife' rather than the generally preferred 'Domestic Duties'. Their two oldest sons Anthony and Henry, aged 11 and 9, were also miners and shared the premises with four younger children. As if this were not enough, there was a lodger as well as William's sister and his niece, who like many women in the village worked at the mill at Linton Falls opened in 1792..

Living in cramped conditions became commonplace. Houses were subdivided to hold more families and every possible spare corner became a building plot, thus putting paid to long gardens running back from the main street that had been such a feature of the village. 'One up one down' and a lean-to were considered adequate for a mining family and overcrowding in the tiniest of dwellings was frequent.

Some households must have seen especially difficult circumstances – and one example is the home of James and Mary Aldersley, both aged 60. This was an advanced number of years for a lead miner but James may well have been working with his son Peter aged 23. The concept that Peter should have moved into his own home then belonged far into the future, as there was simply no accommodation available and the generations stayed together. What singled out the Aldersley home was that it was also occupied by Mary's 33-year old daughter Hannah Dawson, who must have suffered a personal tragedy as she felt obliged to list her occupation as 'Pauper and Miner's Wife'. She would therefore be receiving funds from a charity and no doubt doing her best to look after her son Charles, aged 16, who had also become a miner.

Despite all the difficulties, the overall impression of Grassington in 1851 is of a lively young community with almost half its population aged under 21. It was also wonderfully self-sufficient boasting even more occupations to support the miners than had been the case in 1803. This was especially the case with craftsmen supplying footwear, both for the men and their horses, and thus there were six shoemakers, a clogger, three cordwainers and nine blacksmiths. Other key occupations included five tailors, a barber, four butchers, five bakers and ten carriers. Working with wood had diversified and there was a master carpenter, two cabinetmakers, a master joiner, a French polisher and, perhaps lower down the scale of skills, a broom maker.

Although life was hard, the miners were noted for their sense of fun and excitement. Grassington Feast & Clockmaking became an occasion of much jollity and the most popular institution was a brass band. There was a rival band across the river at Linton and gala days saw each trying to out blow the other. A constant sport was poaching, although presumably the miners recognised that the Duke owned the shooting as well as the mineral rights on the Out Moor and took great care not to be caught.

Playing a crucial role as a setting for local excitement were the four public houses. Staying at the Black Horse on census day were theatre manager William Deville and professor of music Jane Cataline, who were attempting to revive a theatre in the village. It seems they were unsuccessful and it may have been too highbrow for miners, who would no doubt prefer more raucous company in the pub.

This was a situation not at all to the liking of author Bailey Harker, who in his book *Rambles in Upper Wharfedale* lamented that Grassington Mechanics' Institute had failed to counteract the influence of local hostelries as had been hoped. He added: 'The mining population of the town would, any time, rather spend their leisure in shoemakers' shops, or at street corners – where everybody's business and character are discussed, and in a manner not at all creditable – than in places where mental and moral improvement can be gained.' Bailey Harker had strong convictions and became a Congregationalist minister!

The Institute was built by the 6th Duke at his own expense and had as its first president Stephen Eddy, who rose to succeed John Taylor as Mineral Agent. Indicative of his elevated position in the ducal hierarchy were his purpose-built residences of Prospect House (now Colvend) in Grassington and Carleton Grange near Skipton, his home from 1857.

The Devonshire Hotel, one of four public houses in Grassington during mining days. (David Dean collection)

The circular pinfold for stray livestock, which stood at the head of Main Street. Climbing away in the background is the road to Yarnbury. (drawing by John Dean, courtesy David Dean)

In 1855 the pinfold was replaced by Grassington Mechanics' Institute, provided by the 6th Duke at his own expense. Parading past in 1899 is the procession for the traditional May Festival. Three years earlier, ownership had been conveyed to the Parish Council and it became known as the Town Hall. (David Dean collection)

Last throes

These imposing houses marked the end of an era of dynamic expansion, which was symbolised by the deaths in quick succession of the Duke in 1858, Stephen Eddy in 1861 and John Taylor two years later. A familiar story of international changes in the viability of lead extraction, coupled with a failure to find new deposits, meant that output from the Grassington mines was now falling relentlessly. James Ray Eddy followed in his father's footsteps but there was nothing he could do to stem the decline.

A great music lover, he did his best to cheer flagging spirits by forming a miners' choir with himself as conductor. John Lupton, who in his younger days had given out tallow candles to those venturing underground, was taught to play tunes on an old concertina. A piano was even taken onto the moors and the strangest of sights must have been dirt-stained miners rousing the echoes when they took a break between shifts. At the end of a long day they would halt on the way home, assemble in Grassington square and delight the villagers with their massed voices. Eddy became a singer of some renown but his performances in the Mechanics' Institute as 'treats to the work people' can have proved little more than a crumb of comfort.

Only 160 tons of lead was produced in 1871 and the population had fallen to 830. The end was clearly looming and the mines closed in 1882. It must have been a blow to the 7th Duke of Devonshire but was completely overshadowed in the same year by the assassination in Ireland of his son Lord Frederick Cavendish. He became prone to frequent bouts of chronic gloom, his despondency scarcely helped by the fact that growing numbers of steamships were coming into Britain with low-cost imports of foodstuffs as well as lead ore. The Duke's agricultural and mining interests were affected simultaneously and he noted in his diary: 'I am beginning to think large reductions of estate expenditure will soon be necessary as my income is fast falling to a very unpleasant extent.'

One upshot was 'a large company' assembling at Skipton's Devonshire Hotel on 30th June 1886 for an auction of 27 lots of ducal property. Some 2,000 acres of grouse shooting on Grassington Out Moor fetched a respectable £1,520 [£148,000] but the collapse of lead mining had severely depressed the local economy and many properties remained unsold. Future occupants of the area should be thankful that not a single bid was made for the now cherished Grass Wood, despite handbills proclaiming its 'entire suitability for the erection of a Gentleman's Residence, the configuration of the ground offering many eligible and extremely beautiful sites'.

The 7th Duke died in 1891, a year that also saw Grassington reach its lowest-ever population with just 480 inhabitants. As in Swaledale, many mining families had already left and moved to the industrial West Riding and Lancashire. A minority emigrated overseas, this time to Australia as well as North America. It seemed Grassington would become a ghost settlement, but fortunately the scenic attractions

Grassington Square looking decidedly quiet in 1885, three years after closure of the mines. The following year there was a large sale of ducal property and in 1891 the population sunk to below 500 – the lowest ever figure. (David Dean collection)

of the area were just beginning to be more widely known. Ironically, visitors were attracted by the many empty miners' cottages which could be rented for almost nothing – sixpence [£2.40] a week was a common figure – or bought for a few pounds. The railway belatedly arrived in 1902, beginning a period of sustained recovery that ultimately brought prosperity not seen since the early 1850s. Tourists had replaced lead as the driving force.

7. HEBDEN

Less than two miles east of Grassington on the Pateley Bridge turnpike, Hebden had no significant lead mines until as late as the 1850s and yet most of its working men in the first half of the 19th century were miners. In modern terms it was a dormitory village. When cramped living conditions in Grassington became overwhelming, Hebden offered space for the overspill and was no further from the mines. It was also able to offer employment both for girls and older women in a cotton mill opened in 1791.

The village in many ways followed in the footsteps of Grassington and the 1803 muster roll listed 16 miners and two mining agents compared with ten farmers. There was similar despair of the Established Church. In practical terms, worshippers in Hebden had even more reason for dissatisfaction as they were faced with a longer walk to the parish church at Linton. The Methodist chapel, opened in 1812 with space for some 300, eventually prompted the Church of England to provide St Peter's chapel-of-ease in 1841.

The same year's census showed that the village had become a young person's community with 216 out of the 478 inhabitants aged under 15. Ten years later the dormitory role had grown with the proportion of miners exceeding that in Grassington. Hebden had 45 miners, 28 ore dressers and 6 smelters, collectively representing 17 per cent of the population of 466. In Grassington the figure was less than 11 per cent. Yet there were limits in providing space as an overspill village and these had now been reached. Typical of the situation in 1851 was the small terrace home of Thomas and Nancy Hammond, shared with their son John, a lead ore dresser aged 27, and nephew Robert Birch, two years younger and a lead smelter. There were also their four daughters, aged from 29 down to 15 and all working at the mill, as well as a grandson still at school and Nancy's sister Jane who somehow found space to act as servant.

Neither their surroundings nor their neighbours were convivial and Methodist ideals may not have universally succeeded. Referring to Hebden in his *Chronicles and Stories of the Craven Dales*, J.H. Dixon noted that around 1850 the inhabitants were 'little better than savages' and the village was 'a nest of thieves, drunkards and poachers'. Another writer was highly critical of 'a sort of tip, which in warm weather produced an insanitary stench'.

The situation was about to change. Reasonable relations must up to now have

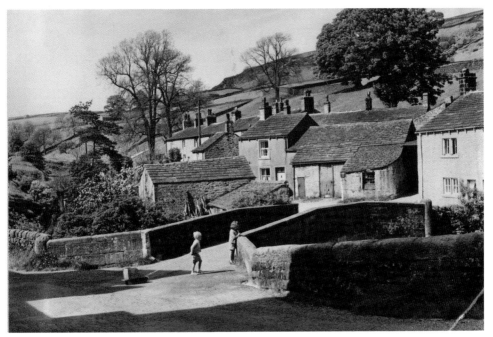

The jumble of houses beyond Hebden's old bridge was largely a product of infilling when miners moved into the village from Grassington. Part of the row on the left was originally an ornate 17th century dwelling of manorial status, which was extended into a terrace and accommodated a large number of miners and mill workers in cramped conditions. (Bertram Unné)

been maintained with the mining hierarchy at Grassington. It can surely have only been John Taylor who in 1840 arranged for William Brown and Henry Daykin to make the lengthy journey from Hebden to assess a mining operation at San Miceli, near Messini in Sicily. Letters penned in tender terms by William to his wife Maria have survived. In one of them he is highly critical of what they found and forecasts that the mine was likely to fail. He may well have been right, as by 1841 they were back in England.

A decade later it seems unlikely that Grassington's mining interests would have been prepared to arrange such a visit, as a bitter dispute culminated in a full-blown lawsuit. Its origins lay in Hebden fundamentally differing from Grassington in that the township rather than a dukedom owned the mineral rights. When in 1589 the Tempest family of Broughton Hall, near Skipton, sold the manor to their tenants they also parted with these rights. The descendants of the tenants, now known as freeholders, had to consent to any search for lead ore within the township. It was a situation that by the early 1850s must have increasingly concerned the 6th Duke's advisors – and especially Stephen Eddy – when some of the most promising Grassington veins pointed in that direction. They attempted to make any lease of the mining rights invalid and no doubt hoped to frighten all concerned by bringing a legal action in the Chancery Court before Baron Cranworth, Lord High Chancellor of Great Britain.

Perhaps to their surprise they did not succeed with the result that in 1856 a 21-year lease was granted to William Sigston Winn, gentleman, of Haverah Park, Harrogate, and five partners all in the West Riding world of wool as merchants or brokers. Trials in Bolton Gill on the northern edge of the township looked distinctly promising with the result that the lease was transferred to the Hebden Moor Mining Company. Tradition holds that Winn sold out for a vast sum, speculated wildly, lost all and returned to England poverty-stricken. Certainly, he was declared bankrupt in 1864 with debts of £1,458 [£128,000] and assets of one gold watch valued at £3 10s [£310].

Bolton Gill operations were at first extremely successful. Conceived when lead mining had reached its zenith, the company was able to benefit from the experience of its predecessors. It had soon sunk a 250ft deep shaft with elaborate pumping, built a dressing floor with the latest mechanical contrivances, constructed its own smelt mill and provided a road down Hebden Gill through what had hitherto been a wild ravine. Inevitably its success was not universally welcomed. Especially troubled was local grocer Francis Hammond, who was also farming over 100 acres [40 hectares] of land including Bolton Gill. He eventually sued the mining company for £300, alleging that 'diverse cows, sheep and goats had fallen into shafts, pits, holes, ditches, channels and watercourses and been drowned, killed, maimed, lamed and injured'.

Yet he was undoubtedly in the minority. Those at the sharp end in the shape of the miners now had their place of work much closer to the village, where most of them lived. An exception who had a house provided close to the dressing floor was the 'Attender to Wheels and Pumps', a colourful job description for what today would be termed a 24/7 responsibility. If the waterwheels stopped turning the mine would not properly function and the lower levels would flood.

In the brief period up to 1862 the company extracted just short of 2,000 tons of ore and realised £27,391 [£2¼ million] in sales of lead. Royalties totalling £3,345 [£280,000] were paid to 45 descendants of the freeholders, bringing to the village both financial benefits and much needed improvements.

High hopes – and calamity

As might be expected, the number of miners in the 1861 census soared to a new high of 93 representing 21 per cent of the 434 inhabitants. This was now way ahead of the proportion in Grassington where mining was already past its peak and greater than in many villages in Swaledale. As elsewhere, there were also

Royalties from mining went directly to village freeholders rather then an absentee landlord. Among several resulting improvements was this new row of terrace housing which included a post office and shop. Overcrowding was thus greatly eased. (Alan Stockdale collection)

men in other occupations directly supporting the miners such as three carters and a blacksmith. An elderly couple, William and Elizabeth Hawley aged 66 and 74, were still keeping alive the ancient craft of knitting stockings. A young coal miner was working shallow seams on the higher reaches of Hebden Gill, enabling the poor quality fuel to be mixed with peat at the smelt mill.

Fortunately the increase in population was more than matched by a growth in the number of households, as part of a determination to ease near impossible living conditions. The terrace home that had been so grossly overcrowded in 1851 now had just three occupants – and this was typical of many. Welfare was improved by the grandly named Star of Hope Lodge of the Independent Order of Oddfellows. It met at the temperance New Inn with the prime object of encouraging workers to provide not just for their own future but also their dependents. A miner joining the lodge at the age of eighteen would incur a monthly subscription of 1s 4d [£5.60] and in the event of illness would receive 9s 0d [£38] per week for up to 52 weeks with £7 [£580] payable on death.

More fundamentally, the decision was taken to re-model the village. A new main street was created, a jumble of farm buildings gave way to substantial houses, and pig sties described as 'anything but a pretty sight' were replaced by a pleasant grass plot. The daily trudge with buckets to get water ceased when a

The third and last attempt to extend mining in the Dales by means of a deep level involved pioneer use of compressed air drilling, powered by this 36ft diameter waterwheel close to the centre of Hebden village. (Janet Stockdale collection)

When work on the deep level was finally abandoned in 1888 the entrance site was acquired by local blacksmith William Bell, seen here outside his forge. Using materials from the mining company, he built an impressive suspension bridge over the River Wharfe which remains in daily use by hundreds of walkers. (Alan Stockdale collection)

piped supply was installed in 1862 and no longer did open drains contribute to Hebden being fever-stricken. In the words of local writer J.A. Bland, it was 'the dawn of a new and brighter day'.

The hope was not to last. In the same year, output of lead ore from Bolton Gill reached its highest annual level of 475 tons but then suddenly stopped. The familiar mining calamity of riches changing into famine hit hard. The veins either became poor or dipped to depths impossible to work within the limits of existing technology. Widening the search by driving additional levels into the side of Hebden Gill failed to find any worthwhile reserves. The population accordingly fell to 361 in the 1871 census but 63 miners remained. This was partly because the wheel had come full circle and they were now back to the longer trek to the Grassington mines, which were still producing small amounts of ore.

Third time unlucky

Even at this late stage the Hebden Moor Mining Company had not given up the elusive quest. In an outburst of supreme optimism it started work on only the third deep level in the Dales. The first Duke's Level, with its entrance little more than a mile up the valley, had successfully extended the life of the Grassington mining field after taking 34 years to complete. The second such venture, Sir Francis Level in Swaledale, was started in 1864 and thanks to more modern methods it reached reserves of ore within 13 years. It must have been well on its way in 1873 when work began on driving the Hebden level that was intended to be both deeper and longer than its predecessors. Starting in the village, it was to extend north-eastwards for almost 1½ miles to enable a 300ft increase in the depth of workings in Bolton Gill.

Despite the pioneer use of compressed air drilling, progress under the guidance of Cornish-born mining agent William Hill was far from rapid. The work was vividly described by the diarist John Henry Wilkinson, when he was taken up the level in 1879 shortly after his visit to Gunnerside:

'Dynamite is placed in the hole bored by the drill; next to the cartridge is placed a strong percussion cap with about 18 inches of fuse, the hole is then filled up with earth and the fuse lighted. It burns perhaps five minutes, giving the men ample time to get out of the reach of the shock, and then ignites. Only two men can work at once; they are relieved every eight hours, and so the work is carried on day and night.'

It continued after 1882, when closure of Grassington's mines should have been the writing on the wall. Not until six years later were rumours of doom apparent when a local newspaper commented: 'Not one ounce of lead is there to show for years of toil and the expenditure of thousands of pounds.' Only two months then elapsed before the company decided it could go no further and yet another vision of finding veins of immense richness proved unfulfilled.

The company went into liquidation and its plant was advertised for sale. William Bell, an enterprising Hebden blacksmith, bought 262 yards of steel rope and used it in building a suspension bridge over the River Wharfe. A stylish grand opening in September 1885, complete with brass band and ample refreshment, must have helped to drown sorrows in a decade marked by general gloom. Hebden's population now fell at its greatest ever rate, declining by a third from 313 to 209 ten years later with 30 houses empty. The village saw closure of one of its two pubs, which with what proved to be a touch of irony had soon after 1875 renamed itself the Jolly Miners.

Only gradually did the position improve and a landmark year was 1902 when wagonettes were able to connect at Grassington station with services on the newly opened Yorkshire Dales Railway from Skipton. West Riding town dwellers soon started to use the train for a day out and an especially popular walk from Grassington up to Yarnbury and down Hebden Gill before returning by the riverside. They must have pondered about all the dereliction at the lead mines but at least Edmund Bogg was able to state in his 1904 book *Two Thousand Miles in Wharfedale*: 'The tide of prosperity is again flowing.'

8. HOLE BOTTOM
A MINING HAMLET

Half a mile north of Hebden is the hamlet of Hole Bottom, where lead miners held sway to an extent never to be found in a larger village. In the total of just three houses were the families of a mine agent, a miner and a smelter. As confessed in the Introduction, it is not just the variety that makes the hamlet especially fascinating to the author. Hole Bottom is where this book has been written and where Joy ancestors have lived since the end of mining days. That aside, researching this chapter has been a rewarding exercise in weaving together many strands from a variety of primary sources. These days so much can be achieved via the Internet and it is small wonder that there has been such a huge growth of interest in family history. Unravelling the saga of these three dwellings will hopefully lead others to undertake a similar exercise with mining settlements. For this reason, the most important sources are listed at the end of this chapter.

Hole Bottom hamlet was not built by miners. When subservience ended in Hebden with sale of the manor in 1598, former tenants became yeomen and gradually moved away from feudal strip farming on common land. A series of small farms with their own homesteads and fields were instead created. At Hole Bottom the three houses had neither name nor number, which mattered little in an age long before bureaucrats and planners. They came to be colloquially known as the Farm, the Cottage and the Stead – an old Dales name for a smallholding. They respectively had 31, 16 and 4 acres of land (12.6, 6.5 and 1.6 hectares), meagre amounts by later standards but quite adequate for the time. In the days before moorland enclosure there was sufficient sheep grazing all the way over to Nidderdale.

The new era of farmers owning and tilling their own land proved to be transient. As elsewhere, the industrial revolution and its sudden demand for lead meant that many became farmer-miners. There was the familiar pattern of dreams of riches round the corner leading to over-spending, with the disastrous result of being forced off the land when mortgages were foreclosed. It happened at Hole Bottom in 1736 when Thomas and Ann Rathmell had to forfeit the Farm. It was sold to William Rishworth of Grassington, who styled himself 'Gentleman' – a man gentle in the sense that he did no manual work and was in a different leagur to a yeoman farmer. He let the farm to a succession of tenants combining farming and mining, beginning with two generations of the Daykin family who came from the Marrick area of Swaledale.

The same trend of owner-occupation giving way to tenanted holdings happened with Hole Bottom Cottage, although in even more unfortunate circumstances. It was inherited by another Ann Rathmell, who in 1767 perhaps made an unwise choice when she married miner John Bownass as her second husband. The following year his cousin came close to the gallows when along with lead-mine labourer and pub landlord Tom Lee, he was charged at York Assizes with the murder of the Grassington doctor, Richard Petty. Bownass was acquitted but Lee was found guilty and hanged before his body was placed in gibbet irons at the scene of the crime in Grass Wood.

Ann died when her sole surviving son was aged only five. Her descendants would experience no difficulty in letting the Cottage over the next hundred years, as with its outbuildings and 16 acres it was a cut above the average miner's home. In the short term it was trustees who let the property to miner James Hallam. It was an age when parish registers often seemed reluctant to recognise women and this was the case at Linton, the then parish church for Hebden. The name of James' wife was never recorded at the baptisms of their nine children in the 1780s and '90s. At least Hole Bottom was now not short of youngsters, as in 1779 a new tenant at the Farm was Grassington miner Thomas Hardacre, who 13 years earlier had married Elizabeth Blackburn. They had six sons and a daughter Nancy and there would be celebrations aplenty in April 1796 at her wedding with Hebden farmer Anthony Joy (the author's great-great-great-grandfather).

Yet happiness has a nasty habit of soon turning to sorrow and only four months later the Hardacres had to leave the Farm. It had been inherited by Thomas Brown, 'Gentleman and Attorney' of Grassington, praised by the haughty Thomas Whitaker in his *History of Craven* as 'worthy and respectable'. The Hardacres may not have shared this view but there would be nothing they could do. The 5th Duke of Devonshire had decided to start work on the massive deep level for his Grassington mines with its entrance only half a mile north of Hole Bottom. It would need constant supervision by a resident agent and the Farm was the perfect base, especially as the land attached to it might yield fresh reserves of lead ore. In August 1796, Thomas Brown accepted a purchase price of £1,950 [£171,000] and the deed was done.

The Hardacres left and 36-year old Thomas Bowdin arrived as agent with his wife Elizabeth, 12 years his younger. Moving from the Duke's copper mine at Ecton cannot have been easy for them. It was like going to a foreign country, as few people then came into the Dales from afar. The population of the time has with some truth been described as the product of centuries of inbreeding.

The Duke strengthened his hold over the hamlet in 1802 by purchasing the

114

Stead, which with its one field had held out as a traditional farm smallholding. It was perhaps inevitable that future tenants should be tied to the Grassington mines with Thomas Worsley and his successors working at the Cupola smelt mill. For almost the next thirty years Hole Bottom had its three homesteads housing the families of agent, miner and smelter, but to what extent they relished one another's presence must for ever be a matter of conjecture.

Tragedy in the wings

Death and misfortune were never far away. In 1800 James Hallam died at the Cottage leaving eight surviving children under the age of 18. The new occupants were miner Robert Birch and his wife Jane, who not unusually for the time saw three of their six children die before reaching adulthood. Subsequent events can have done little to improve the local clergy's low regard for the morals of lead miners.

The oldest son Jonathan survived to become a miner and spent much of his time in the village with his uncle John, whose daughter Ann was just three years younger. He got to know her very well indeed and by May 1810 she was pregnant. A Birch thus married a Birch three months later and they decided to live in Hebden where their daughter Isabella was born in February 1811. There were funerals later that year for Jonathan's brother and then on 15th December

Hole Bottom hamlet looking up Hebden Gill. The crags on the distant hill overlook Bolton Gill, where rich deposits of lead ore were found in the mid-1850s. (W.E. Leadley)

115

Hole Bottom Farm, much as it looked when sold by the 7th Duke of Devonshire in 1886. The 5th Duke had bought the property 90 years earlier as a suitable home for Thomas Bowdin, appointed as agent to oversee building of the deep level half a mile up the valley.

1813 for his father Robert. To say the least, family mourning was brief. Shortage of affordable housing in the Dales is nothing new and it was then so acute that just five days later miner Stephen Birch married pregnant Margaret Harling and immediately moved into the Cottage to share it with widowed Jane. Their son, another Robert, was born the following April and they had a further five children in the next eleven years.

Somehow they all managed to squeeze into the two-bedroom property until Jane's death in 1823. They then moved into Hebden and were succeeded by another miner Joseph Hudson, who the previous Boxing Day had married Elizabeth Arstingstall – born in Aysgarth and possessing an extraordinary maiden name verging on the impolite. They soon had three children.

There was again no lack of youngsters at Hole Bottom, as over at the Farm the Bowdins had seven sons and three daughters in the 14 years following their move north. Several of the sons became miners and fostered musical tradition by forming an orchestra. Craven Museum in Skipton still has the 'Instructions for Violincelle' [violoncello], signed by the eldest son Daniel. These were good times, coinciding with revival of the Grassington mines ending a long period of

Hole Bottom Cottage was not on the same scale as the Farm but was still a cut above the abode of the average miner. It was thus rarely unoccupied with two adults plus six or more children somehow being crammed into its two bedrooms.

gloom and poor employment prospects.

The orchestra would no doubt perform at its finest at a series of Bowdin weddings from 1818 onwards. The fifth of them involving the marriage of miner Henry Bowdin to Jane Brayshaw, daughter of a local inn-keeper, took place in November 1828. Their daughter Elizabeth was baptised a month later but was never to be aware of her father. Henry died in February 1829 at the age of only 23 and tragedy was now heaped on tragedy. In April the depleted family had again to gather at the graveside for the burials of his brothers Richard, aged 25, and Orlando, only 16. That was not all. The Bowdins no doubt continued to see much of fellow miner Jonathan Birch following his move from the Cottage to the village in 1810. In the space of just two weeks in the same fatal months of 1829 the deaths occurred of Jonathan, his daughter Isabella, aged 18, and much younger son George who was just seven.

The cause of all these young deaths remains unknown. It was certainly no massive epidemic, as mortality rates in Hebden were not above average and indeed after Orlando's burial in mid-April there were only two further funerals at Linton church until the following August. A TV drama would hold that Henry

Bowdin and Jonathan Birch had been working together in appalling conditions down the same mine and contracted infectious pneumonia or tuberculosis with terrible consequences for their families.

An equivalent of the *Poldark* saga and its Cornish tin miners would no doubt also make much of what happened to Jonathan's surviving son Joseph, orphaned at the age of 16. After a period as a lead ore dresser, he left Hebden in the 1830s to indulge in what his descendants described as 'a complex life'. He eventually said his goodbyes and headed for America and Grant County, Wisconsin, with its thriving lead mines. After a year his first wife Sarah set sail to join him with her two stepsons and step-daughter, the eldest son Samuel much later penning a journal that makes stirring reading. Sarah died midway through the 30-day voyage and had to be buried at sea, leaving three children aged between three and ten to fend for themselves. Cared for in New York, they were ultimately reunited with their father and the family became involved in silver and gold prospecting before founding the village of Birchnall in Iowa. Joseph lived far longer than might have been the case had he not emigrated and died at the age of 89.

Changing fortunes
Back in the Birch family homeland, Hole Bottom never fully recovered from the tragic events of 1829. At the Farm, Thomas Bowdin was almost 70 when just after Christmas 1834 he drew up his will, dividing his small share in Coniston Copper Mines among his remaining family and leaving his mineral books and specimens specifically to his eldest son and miner Daniel. After his death the following July and the marriage of his youngest daughter, the only occupants of a home that had once echoed to the music and laughter of a dozen folk were his widow, two sons – neither of whom were actively employed in mining – and Henry's orphaned daughter.

Over at the Cottage, the occupants ceased to be miners after more than half a century when the Hudsons moved out and members of the Hardacre family of farmers took their place. Only at the Stead was there some continuity with William, the eldest son of smelter Thomas Worsley, having married Ellen Birbeck in 1822. Running in front of the house was Paradise Beck and it was perhaps inevitable that an enduring legend should grow up round their two youngest children Jane and Adam, born in 1829 and 1831. Jane got the nickname Eve and the fable told of Adam and Eve romping among thorns and thistles in the garden of Eden – alias Ellen – reached from Hebden by going uphill to Paradise,

William had followed in his father's footsteps by becoming a smelter, as did his oldest son George, but change was again soon on the horizon. The Worsleys left in the early 1840s and their home was allowed to fall into ruin, leaving little more than foundations that today are an archaeological project. It must have seemed that the last link between the hamlet and lead mining was ending. Yet there was destined to be a final fling, the 1851 census showing that the Hardacres had left the Cottage and the new occupants were a classic mining family.

Head of the household was Thomas Wiggan, whose wife Ann was from Swaledale. This other great stronghold of Dales mining was still a world away and the census enumerator struggled with the correct spelling, recording her birthplace as 'Muca' rather than Muker. Thomas and their first four sons, including the youngest aged only nine, were all lead ore dressers. They would initially follow in the footsteps of previous generations of Hole Bottom miners and tramp over the moors to Yarnbury and the Grassington mines, although it would surely have made sense for them to transfer to the new dressing floor of the Hebden Moor Mining Company when it began operations in 1856. It was after all little more than half a mile away and could easily be reached by a new cart road constructed up the valley and rendering obsolete the old track that had climbed past the Stead.

Yet it was to the Duke's Mineral Agent, James Ray Eddy, that Thomas Wiggan turned when he received an unwelcome letter in November 1868. For the first time since it had been built some two centuries earlier, the Cottage was put up for sale. A descendant of Ann Rathmell wrote to give Thomas first refusal to buy the house and its attached land for £1,050 [£84,500]. He was asked to reply by return but a fundamental problem was that like much of the mining population he was unable to write. Eddy and Thomas therefore met the vendor with the result that it was the Mineral Agent who promptly acquired the property. His motives may not have been altruistic, as he would now have entitlement to a share of royalties from the Hebden mines and a say in any future workings that might adversely affect his Grassington operations.

Such hopes were never fulfilled and the rapid decline in lead mining meant that Hole Bottom soon became a ghost hamlet. By the 1881 census Thomas was there on his own as a 71-year old farmer looking after his 16 acres, all his family having moved away with second son Henry founding Wiggan's Evangelistic Mission in London. Across at the Farm there was just Horatio, fifth son of Thomas Bowdin, with Elizabeth – orphaned daughter of Henry – acting as housekeeper.

The final curtain started to fall in 1886 when the 7th Duke of Devonshire included the Farm in his batch of Grassington and other property put up for auction in Skipton. James Ray Eddy had hopes of adding it to the Cottage and land he had already acquired, but his highest bid of £1,500 [£146,000] was unsuccessful. It was instead knocked down for £2,050 [£200,000] to farmers David and Richard Joy, grandsons of the Anthony Joy who 90 years earlier had married Nancy from the Hole Bottom family of Hardacres. The wheel had come full circle and the hamlet's mining heyday had lasted less than a century.

The last tenuous link was broken when the mental health of James Ray Eddy started to fail and he reputedly burnt large quantities of mining records still in his office. He was admitted to The Retreat at York where he died of 'senile decay' in November 1918, aged 85. It was somehow symbolic of the end of an era that his estate was left to the mercies of three spinster sisters in Torquay, who promptly arranged its disposal

Consulted in writing this chapter

Parish Registers for Linton-in-Craven. Those for the years 1562 to 1812 have been published in two volumes by the Yorkshire Archaeological Society – Parish Register Section (YPRS Vols 5 and 18). The second volume (1779 – 1812) is available online: www.archive.org/details/registersofparis18lint. Registers for the period 1813 – 1958 have been put on a CD by Wharfedale Family History Group (www.wharfedalefhg.org.uk)

Registry of Deeds, West Yorkshire County Record Office, Wakefield (WYCRO).

Land Tax Assessments for Hebden, 1760 and 1782 to 1832 (WYCRO).

Hebden Tithe Award and Map 1846/7, North Yorkshire County Record Office, Northallerton.

Census returns, 1841 to 1891.

Help received from the following is gratefully acknowledged:
Members of Hebden Hisory Group
Anthony Bowdin (family details are on: www.odassociates.plus.com/bowdin)
Rev David Birch for supplying the journal of Samuel Birch – published in Grant County Heritage Vol 17 Nos 1 – 4 (May 1993 to February 1994).
Mike & Lyn Worsley.

GONE BUT NOT FORGOTTEN

Men of lead have long gone from the Yorkshire Dales but their presence never seems far away. Whether it be the hundreds of abandoned mine levels, or the spectacular hushes of Gunnerside Gill, or more dramatic reminders such as the striking smelt-mill chimney high on Grassington Moor, the past has not been erased.

The remains are in quiet places. At many a former dressing floor the only sound is running water tumbling down the fellside, punctuated by the occasional bleat of a sheep and the calls of moorland birds. In the silence it is not difficult to imagine former times.

A pony, led by a young lad, is towing loaded tubs out of the level. Many men – and some women – are sorting and washing the ore. A blacksmith's hammer clangs as picks are sharpened. There is much shouting in order to be heard above the hiss and shudder of a constantly turning waterwheel and the noise of a grinding mill and hotching tubs. A more distant wheel is pumping the mine where far down in the eerie darkness is just the drip, drip of water as miners toil by the light of a tallow candle.

At one end of the dressing floor, ore is being piled into carts and taken down to the smelting mill. Here a smelt is underway and a chimney is belching black smoke and poisonous fumes. The bellows are working hard and molten lead is about to flow. Outside the mill, more carts have been loaded with precious lead and set off on the long journey to a distant canal, where progress will be a little but not a lot faster.

On their way along a miners' track they pass groups of men tramping to start a six or eight-hour shift. They are singing, as music is in their soul and is part of an indomitable spirit that survives poverty, uncertainty and danger. It would certainly never cross the minds of these men that they and their achievements would still be regarded with awe in the 21st century. They achieved so much for so little and left a legacy that should be a source of pride. May they never be forgotten.

SOURCES AND FURTHER READING

General

Bishop, Janet, *'Women and Mining Communities in the Dales'*, in British Mining No. 92 (Northern Mine Research Society, 2011).

Bowes, Peter & Roberts, Arthur, *'Farmer-miners of the High Pennines'*, in Optima, Vol 31, No 4 (December 1983)

Clough, Robert T., *The Lead Smelting Mills of the Yorkshire Dales* (Author, 1962)

Dickinson, J.M., *A History of Lead Mining in Airedale, Wharfedale and Nidderdale* (Author, 1972)

Gill, M.C. & Burt, R., *The Mines of Yorkshire* (Northern Mine Research Society, 2003)

Hartley, Marie & Ingilby, Joan, *Life and Tradition in the Yorkshire Dales* (Dent, 1968)

Hunt, C.J., *The Lead Miners of the Northern Pennines in the eighteenth and nineteenth centuries* (Manchester University Press, 1970) [Teesdale to the Tyne Valley]

Joy, David (compiler), *Arthur Raistrick's Yorkshire Dales* (Dalesman, 1991) [especially *'Life in the Lead Mines'* pp 144-150 and *'Spirit of the Dales'* pp 153-4]

Morrison, John, *Lead Mining in the Yorkshre Dales* (Dalesman, 1998) [general introduction with walks]

Raistrick, Arthur, *Lead Mining in the Mid-Pennines* (Bradford Barton, 1973)

Raistrick, Arthur & Jennings, Bernard, *A History of Lead Mining in the Pennines* (Longmans, 1965)

Raistrick, Arthur & Roberts, Arthur, *Life and Work of the Northern Lead Miner* (Beamish Museum and Northern Mine Research Society, 1984) [photo album primarily covering from Teesdale to the Tyne Valley]

Walton, James, *Homesteads of the Yorkshire Dales* (Dalesman, 1947)

Swaledale

Bagenal, T.B., *Miners and Farmers* (Northern Mine Research Society, 1999) [agricultural holdings of lead miners at Heights, Gunnerside]

Barker, J.L., *'The Lead Miners of Swaledale and Arkengarthdale in 1851'*, in Memoirs of the Northern Cavern & Mine Research Society (Vol 2, No 2, August 1972)

Batty, Margaret, *Gunnerside Chapel and Gunnerside Folk* (Author, 1972)

Cooper, Edmund, *A History of Swaledale* (Dalesman, 1973)

Cooper, Edmund, Muker: *The Story of a Yorkshire Parish* (Dalesman, 1948; Hayloft Publishing, 2010)

Fawcett, Edward R. (edit. Lee, Brian), *Lead Mining in Swaledale* (Faust Publishing, 1985).

Fieldhouse, R. & Jennings, B., *A History of Richmond and Swaledale* (Phillimore, 1978)

Gill, M.C., *Swaledale – its Mines and Smelt Mills* (Landmark, 2001)

Hallas, Christine, *Rural Responses to Industrialization: The North Yorkshire Pennines 1790-1914* (Peter Lang, Bern, 1999) [Wensleydale and Swaledale]

Hardy, John, *Swaledale – Portrait of a North Yorkshire Mining Community* (Frank Peters, 1998) [high production values and illustrations but heavily criticised for an inaccurate text]

Hartley, Marie & Ingilby, Joan, *The Old Hand-Knitters of the Dales* (Dalesman, 1951)

Hartley, Marie & Ingilby, Joan, *A Dales Heritage* (Dalesman, 1982) [especially chapters 5 on the Beldi Hill dispute and 8 on the Stockton lead and shipping agent]

Hatcher, Jane, *Richmondshire Architecture* (Author, 1990)

Jackson, Thomas Hayes, *'Diseases of Miners of Arkendale and Swaledale'*, in British Medical Journal (No. xxx, 25th July 1857)

Mills,Alan, *Mining and Miners in 19th Century Swaledale and Arkengarthdale* (Friends of the Swaledale Museum, 2006)

Morris, David, *The Dalesmen of the Mississippi River* (William Sessions, 1989) [the emigration of Swaledale miners]

Pontefract, Ella, *Swaledale* (Dent, 1934)

Pratt, Mildred Claire, *The Silent Ancestors* (McClelland and Stewart, Toronto, 1971). [the Pratt family of Gunnerside]

Raistrick, Arthur, *The Lead Industry of Wensleydale and Swaledale*, Vol 1 The Mines, Vol 2 The Smelting Mills (Moorland, 1975)

Sweetmore, Keith, *'Out of court: the battle for Beldi Hill'*, in British Mining No 92 (Northern Mine Research Society, 2011)

Tyson, L.O., *The Arkengarthdale Mines* (Northern Mine Research Society, 1995)

Tyson, L.O., *A History of the Manor and Lead Mines of Marrick, Swaledale* (Northern Mine Research Society, 1989)

Tyson, LO., *'Mining at Hurst'*, in The Dalesman, Vol 48, No. 7 (October 1986)

Tyson, L.O. & Spensley, R.M. with White, R.F., *The Grinton Mines* (Northern Mine Research Society, 1995)

Greenhow

Ashley Cooper, Anne, *Yorke Country* (Author, 1988)

Gill, M.C., *The Greenhow Mines* (Northern Mine Research Society, 1998)

Greenhow History Club, *Life on the Hill – Greenhow: Its mining history, people and way of life* (2005)

Jennings, Bernard (edit), *A History of Nidderdale* (Advertiser Press, 1967)

Grassington

Brooks, Susan D., *A History of Grassington* (Dalesman, 1979)

Burt, Roger, *John Taylor – mining entrepreneur and engineer 1779-1863* (Moorland, 1977)

Gill, M.C., *'John Barratt and the Grassington Mines 1818 – 1834'*, in Bulletin of the Peak District Mines Historical Society (Vol 17, No 6, Winter 2010).

Gill, M.C., *The Grassington Mines* (Northern Mine Research Society, 1993)

Gill, M.C, *'Women's Place in Lead Mining at Grassington'*, in British Mining No. 88 (Northern Mine Research Society, 2009)

Pearson, John, *Stags and Serpents: the story of the House of Cavendish* (Macmillan, 1983).

Raistrick, Arthur, *Old Yorkshire Dales* (David & Charles, 1967) [chap 11 – 'A parish in 1851' (Linton)]

Whitaker, Thomas Dunham, *The History and Antiquities of the Deanery of Craven* (republished E.J.Morten and the Craven Herald, 1973)

Hebden and Hole Bottom

Gill, M.C., *The Wharfedale Mines* (Northern Mine Research Society, 1994)

Joy, David, *Hebden – The History of a Dales Township* (Hebden History Group, 2002)

Joy, David, *Uphill to Paradise – The Story of Hole Bottom hamlet* (Author, 1991)

Other areas

Gill, M.C. & Squirrell, Mike, *The Malham Mines* (Northern Mine Research Society, 2014)

Spensley, I.M., *Mines and Miners of Wensleydale* (UK Book Publishing, 2014)

INDEX

Illustrations in bold type

125

PEOPLE